Easy Peasy Language Arts 2 Parent's Guide

Welcome to the EP Language Arts 2 Parent's Guide!

This little book was created to help you go offline while following EP's Language Arts 2 curriculum. You will need the Language Arts 2 Workbook for your child. Without the online lessons, you will need to be your child's teacher. The directions are here for introducing new topics. The workbook will provide practice and review.

This book also includes objectives for each lesson, materials marked where needed, directions for what to do each lesson, and the complete answer key.

This course covers all language arts topics including: writing, grammar, handwriting, and spelling. Please realize that every piece of copywork is working on those things as they form the words of well-written sentences. Those sentences all come from books in our EP Second Reader. Throughout the year students will be writing creatively and, at the end of the year, producing a non-fiction paragraph and book.

A little note: To avoid calling all children "he" or the awkward phrasing of "him or her," I've used the plural pronoun when referring to your child, such as, "Brainstorm with your child words that rhyme with tree, and see how many they can come up with."

Have a great year.

Lee

Note: We used to call each lesson a day: "Day 1," "Day 2," etc. We've replaced those days with "lessons," but you'll see "day" still in the mini pages in the answer section. Those pages are the same, not outdated, just that one word is changed.

Lesson 1

- Students will: use phonics to build words
- Lesson 1 worksheet
  - They can try the different word segments in the box along with the beginning of the word in the sentence to see what makes sense.

Lesson 2

- Students will: write a descriptive sentence.
- Lesson 2 worksheet
  - There's a picture of tongs. There's a sentence starter at the top of the page.

Lesson 3

- Students will: write a persuasive sentence.
- Lesson 3 worksheet
  - There is a topic on their page, treating animals kindly.

Lesson 4

- Students will: write a humorous sentence.
- Lesson 4 worksheet
  - They are to write a nonsense sentence.

Lesson 5 (red and blue crayons/colored pencils)

- Students will: identify common and proper nouns, edit capitalization in incorrect sentences.
  - Review proper and common nouns.
    - When nouns are names, they are called **proper nouns** and are always capitalized. They always start with a capital letter. Some examples: name of a person, Mary; name of a place, California; name of a thing, Oreos. If the noun is a name and starts with a capital letter, it is proper. If it doesn't, then we call it just a **common** noun.
    - Together come up with examples of names of people, places, and things. Those are all proper nouns.
  - Ask your child what else needs to be capitalized besides names.
    - the first letter in each sentence
- Lesson 5 worksheet
  - They will color red the common nouns and blue the proper nouns.
  - They will underline the words that should be capitalized.

Lesson 6 (scissors)

- Students will: identify contractions
- Review contractions.
  - o Remember, a contraction is a shorter way of saying something. Can't means can not. She'll means she will.
  - o Have your child figure out the shorter way of saying, "I am coming."
    - ▪ I'm coming.
- Lesson 6 worksheet
  - o They should read the page before it is cut up. Each contraction is next to its meaning.
  - o Then these squares should be cut up and placed faced down to play Memory/Concentration.

Lesson 7

- Students will: write a story
- Lesson 7 worksheet
  - o There is a writing prompt on the page. They can get started by copying it.

Lesson 8

- Students will: identify correct sentences, write correct sentences
- Ask your child what every sentence begins and ends with.
  - o a capital letter, ending punctuation: period, question mark, exclamation point
- Lesson 8 worksheet
  - o They will choose which sentence is correct.
  - o They will rewrite the sentences to make them correct.

Lesson 9

- Students will: copy lines of a poem, use transition words to order directions
- Lesson 9 worksheet
  - o First, they will copy the lines of the poem on the page.
  - o Second, they should read through all of the directions before they begin ordering them.
    - ▪ They need to notice the jelly goes on the peanut butter, so the peanut butter has to go on first.

Lesson 10

- Students will: identify which words in a sentence need capitalizing, write sentences with correct capitalization
- Review proper nouns, names of people, places, and things.
  - o Ask your child if they should capitalize Monday.

- ▪ Yes, it's the name of a day of the week.
  - o Ask your child if they should capitalize December.
    - ▪ Yes, it's the name of a month.
  - o Ask your child if they should capitalize Walmart.
    - ▪ Yes, it's the name of a store.
- Lesson 10 worksheet
  - o They will underline the words that need to be capitalized and then write out the sentences with correct capitalization.

Lesson 11

- Students will: create compound words
- Review compound words.
  - o Sometime is an example of a compound word. Some + Time = sometime
  - o Rainbow is another example of a compound word. Rain + bow = rainbow
- Lesson 11 worksheet
  - o They will put the beginnings and endings of the words together. They can read the parts together until one makes sense.

Lesson 12

- Students will: copy lines of poem, identify rhyming words
- Lesson 12 worksheet
  - o They will copy the lines and then write the rhyming words.

Lesson 13

- Students will: copy the lines of a poem, correct capitalization and ending punctuation
- Lesson 13 worksheet
  - o At the top of the page is copywork.
  - o The second part has them underline what needs to be capitalized and add in the ending punctuation.

Lesson 14

- Students will: copy lines of a poem, identify rhyming words
- Read the lines of the poem for your child.
  - o Stroke a flint, and there is nothing to admire: Strike a flint, and forthwith flash out sparks of fire.
  - o Explain what a flint is and what the poem means.
  - o Point out how "stroke a flint" and "strike a flint" are repeating phrases, even though they aren't identical. They set up the poem to compare the two different ways you can handle a flint.
- Lesson 14 worksheet
  - o They will copy the lines and write the rhyming words.

Lesson 15

- Students will: write a rhyming poem
- Have your child think of words that rhyme with wig.
  - There are some listed on the Lesson 15 worksheet page.
- Lesson 15 worksheet
  - There is part of a sentence on the page, "If a pig wore a wig,…"
  - They can copy that and then finish the sentence, ending with a word that rhymes with wig.

Lesson 16
- Students will: copy lines of poetry, recognize that some words don't change in the plural
- Review plural words with your child.
  - A plural word is talking about more than one. Quiz your child.
    - one bike, two _____ (bike<u>s</u>)
    - one shelf, five _____ (shel<u>ves</u>)
    - one box, many _____ (box<u>es</u>)
    - one moose, three _____ (moose)
  - Some words don't change in the plural. Some of those words are on their worksheet for today.
- Lesson 16 worksheet
  - Copy lines of poetry.
  - Write the plural of the words. None of them change.

Lesson 17
- Students will: write rhymes, write two lines of rhyming poetry following a given pattern
- Lesson 17 worksheet
  - Read the poem together that's on their worksheet page.
  - They will write two lines using the pattern in the poem. Here's an example.
    - What is red? My blanket's red, lying on my bed.
  - They can use the color rhymes at the bottom of the page for ideas.

Lesson 18
- Students will: identify and write correct plurals
- Practice plurals:
  - one book, two _____ (book<u>s</u>)
  - one wolf, five _____ (wol<u>ves</u>)
  - one fox, many _____ (fox<u>es</u>)
    - Words that end with X, SH, CH, or SS get an ES added onto them to make them plural. (On their page is the word fish. It ends with SH, but we don't change it, two fish.)
  - one lunch, many _____ (lunch<u>es</u>)
  - one deer, three _____ (deer)

- Lesson 18 Worksheet
  - o First they will just choose the correct plural.
  - o Second they will have to write the plural. If they ask you about one, read them the rules instead of just telling them the answer.

Lesson 19
- Students will: read poetry and identify rhymes and repetition, write a poem with rhyme and repetition
- Lesson 19 worksheet
  - o Read the poem together.
  - o They will identify the rhymes and repeated words.
  - o They can make their own poem in the pattern demonstrated, or they can use my line as a writing prompt to get them started.

Lesson 20 (scissors)
- Students will: copy a stanza of poetry, identify irregular plurals
- Lesson 20 worksheet
  - o There is copywork, a stanza of poetry. A stanza is like a paragraph of poetry.
  - o The boxes on the page need to be cut out. Then your child can lay them upside down and play Memory/Concentration and find the matches.

Lesson 21
- Students will: use phonics to complete words by writing in two-letter blends
- Lesson 21 worksheet
  - o Encourage your child to read the word with each ending on it to listen for what makes sense.

Lesson 22
- Students will: practice their spelling words
- Lesson 22 worksheet
  - o They will use the list of words to search for them in the word search. The words only go down or across. Nothing is diagonal or backwards.
  - o Play hangman. The word is grand.
    - ▪ They have five blanks on their page. Have your child guess letters and you write them in as they guess them. You don't have to draw a hangman.

Lesson 23
- Students will: practice their spelling words
- Lesson 23 worksheet
  - o They will unscramble the words and write them in the sentence blanks.
    - ▪ They should read a sentence and think about what would fit there and then look for that in the list of words.
    - ▪ If your child gets really stuck, they can turn back to the previous two pages which have the lists of words.

Lesson 24
- Students will: spell words without visual cues
- Have a spelling bee.
  - Have your child spell these words out loud.
    - pond, lost, grand, past, rust
- Lesson 24 worksheet
  - The rest of their words are on their page. They will fill in the blanks with the spelling word that fits. They should use the words they've been practicing.

Lesson 25
- Students will: be assessed on their spelling, identify nouns
- Lesson 25 worksheet
  - Read your child the spelling words one at a time. Don't give any clues. You can put it in a sentence if that helps them.
    - cast, grand, rust, lost, sand, past, hand, list, pond, nest
  - There are several words at the bottom of the page. They can circle the nouns.
    - Nouns are people, places, or things.

Lesson 26
- Students will: copy a line of literature and then create their own in the same format
- Lesson 26 worksheet
  - First they will copy the sentence.
  - Then they will fill in their own adjective and what it describes.
    - Here's an example.
      - It is a very exciting thing when we have our first warm day, very exciting indeed.
    - You can brainstorm adjectives together: mysterious, brave, sad, silly,…

Lesson 27
- Students will: copy a line of literature and then create their own in the same format
- Lesson 27 worksheet
  - First they will copy the sentence.
  - Then they will fill in their own ideas.
    - Here's an example.
      - You know my dog is always ready to dig or do anything that will make her dirty.
    - Have them start with a person or animal and then have them think about what that person or animal would do.

Lesson 28 (book, They are to look for four plural words.)
- Students will: write plural and singular nouns
- Ask your child what the regular way is to make a word plural. How does bike become bikes or book become books?
  - You just need to add an S.
- Lesson 28 worksheet
  - They will write the plural or the singular form of the nouns. They all are regular plurals, just add S.
  - Then they will need to write in four plurals of their own. They can make them up if they don't have a book to copy them from.

Lesson 29
- Students will: copy a line of literature and then create their own in the same format
- Lesson 29 worksheet
  - First they will copy the sentence.
  - Then they will fill in their own ideas.
    - Here's an example.
      - Sometimes I envy birds because they can fly and soar in the sky.
    - Have them start by choosing an animal and then think about what's special about the animal that they would like to be able to do.
  - There are no commas in these sentences.

Lesson 30
- Students will: write plural forms of singular nouns
- Lesson 30 worksheet
  - Read the rules over together.
    - Make sure your child knows the difference between a vowel (A, E, I, O, U) and a consonant for the Y becomes I rule.
      - boy, boys
      - try, tries
  - Encourage your child to use them to write the plurals.

Lesson 31
- Students will: copy a quotation and write a question
- Lesson 31 worksheet
  - They will copy the sentence. Make sure they copy the quotation marks and question mark.
  - They will write their own question. It must end in a question mark.

Lesson 32
- Students will: copy and write an exclamation
- Lesson 32 worksheet
  - They will copy the sentence. Make sure they copy the commas and that it ends with an exclamation point.
  - They will write their own exclamation, like they are excited about something, warning about something, or shouting something.

Lesson 33
- Students will: copy a quotation and write a question
- Lesson 33 worksheet
  - They will copy the sentence. Make sure they copy the quotation marks and question mark.
  - They will write their own question. It must end in a question mark.

Lesson 34
- Students will: copy and write an exclamation
- Lesson 34 worksheet
  - They will copy the sentence. Make sure they copy the commas and that it ends with an exclamation point.
  - They will write their own exclamation with quotation marks. There is an example on the page for them to see how the sentence is structured.
    - They can start with quotation marks and then something they would say in an excited voice.
    - Next comes the exclamation point and then more quotation marks.
    - Finally they will write who was talking, I said, or something like that.

Lesson 35
- Students will: identify nouns including ideas as nouns
- Lesson 35 worksheet
  - Read through the top of the page together. Ideas or feelings as "things" is new for them, things like fear and love and happiness.

Lesson 36
- Students will: write words with the AR phonics sound
- Today the words they will write will all have the AR sound as in car. Together with your child rhyme words with car.
- You can also think of other AR words, such as barn and farm.
- Lesson 36 worksheet
  - They will read the sentences and write the words from the box in the blanks.

Lesson 37
- Students will: write words with the ER phonics sound
- The ER sound in a word can be spelled ER, IR, or UR.
- Together with your child think of ER words. Here are some: purr, burn, burp.
- Lesson 37 worksheet
  - They will read the sentences and write the words from the box in the blanks.
  - Then they will try to write some other words.

Lesson 38
- Students will: identify proper nouns, correct capitalization of proper nouns
- Review what a proper noun is: a noun that is the name of a person, place, or thing. Come up with examples of names of people, places, and things.
  - George Washington
  - California
  - Disney World
- Lesson 38 worksheet
  - They will find and circle the proper nouns that are incorrectly written with a lowercase letter.
  - Then they will write the proper nouns in the blanks with a capital letter.

Lesson 39
- Students will: write words with OR
- Lesson 39 worksheet
  - Look at the pictures on the page together and name the OR words using the pictures.
    - fork, corn, horn, cork
  - Can you think of any other OR words together?
    - born, word, fort, torn

Lesson 40
- Students will: write I words, identify nouns
- Lesson 40 worksheet
  - Take a look at the page together.
  - Look at the words at the top of the page. Point out to your child the different ways to write the I sound.
  - At the bottom of the page they will find the nouns.

Lesson 41
- Students will: write words with –ARE spelling pattern, identify proper nouns
- Come up with words together that have the –ARE spelling pattern.
  - bare, scare, fare, mare, rare, pare, care, dare, hare, ware
- Lesson 41 worksheet
  - They will write –ARE words in the blanks on the page.
  - They will circle the proper nouns. They all start with a capital letter.

Lesson 42 (orange crayon)
- Students will: identify rhyming words and words with the AIR spelling pattern
- Together with your child think of words that rhyme with chair.
- Lesson 42 worksheet
  - They will find words that rhyme with chair and write one of the "air" words in the blank on the page.

Lesson 43
- Students will: identify and write common and proper nouns
- Review common and proper nouns. Common nouns are people, places, and things, and proper nouns are the names of people, places, and things.
- Lesson 43 worksheet
  - The students will identify the nouns as common or proper.
  - Then they should write common and proper nouns. Encourage your child to come up with new ones if they can instead of copying.

Lesson 44 (red and brown crayons)
- Students will: identify words with the OY phonics sound
- Together come up with words that have the OY sound.
  - joy, noise, coin, boing, boys
- Lesson 44 worksheet
  - The students will color in red the words with the OY sound.
  - They will write their name, phone number, and address. You'll have to help with that probably.

Lesson 45
- Students will: write words with the OW sound, identify common and proper nouns
- Together come up with words with the OW sound.
  - cloud, crown, brown, sound, etc.
- Lesson 45 worksheet
  - They will use the sentences and word box to fill in the crossword puzzle. Make sure they know how to find the numbers and fill it in.
  - Then they will follow the directions to identify the common and proper nouns.

Lesson 46 (optional: colored pencils or crayons for drawing a picture)
- Students will: write words with the AW sound
- Try to come up with words that rhyme with paw and claw. Try to avoid words that end in L. You can over pronounce the L at the end of words like ALL to show how they have a different ending.
- Lesson 46 worksheet
  - They will use the words in the box to figure out what word goes in each sentence.
  - Then there's a spot for them to draw a picture.

Lesson 47
- Students will: write words with the AL sound
- Together come up with words that rhyme with ALL. Emphasize the L sound to help them distinguish it from AW. They are going to be writing words with Ls in them.
  - For instance, ball, call, fall, mall, …
- Lesson 47 worksheet
  - They will use the words in the box to write the appropriate word in each blank.
  - Then there is a word search and a place to write three rhyming words.

Lesson 48
- Students will: identify and write common and proper nouns, practice common and proper noun capitalization rules
- Review nouns.
  - Ask your child what is a noun.
    - It's a person, place, thing, or idea or feeling (love, fear, happiness).
  - Ask your child what's the difference between a common and proper noun.
    - A common noun is a person, place, or thing, but a proper noun is a name of a person, place, or thing.
- Lesson 48 worksheet
  - They will have to identify the common and proper nouns in the sentences.
  - Then they will have to write common and proper nouns. Make sure that the common nouns start with a lowercase letter and that the proper nouns start with a capital letter.

Lesson 49
- Students will: order the story, identify words with the long A sound
- Together think of words with the long A sound. Here are some to get you started.
  - rain, mail, age
  - You can use those to think of rhymes, but you can also think of your own words.
- Lesson 49 worksheet
  - They will read the story. It might be easiest to read it out loud. If they notice any words with a long A sound, they should underline them.
  - Then they will number the pictures to show the order they happened in the story.

Lesson 50
- Students will: write ING words, write sentences
- Together think of words that rhyme with sing.
  - For instance: wing, ring, spring, fling, bring…
  - Each of those words ends with ING. That makes the ING sound.
  - We use ING with lots of verbs like running, jumping, talking, singing, finding, laughing, …

- Lesson 50 worksheet
    - They will use the picture to figure out what ING word they need to write.
    - Then they will write four sentences. They can use the words at the top of the page or their own ING words.

Lesson 51
- Students will: write INK words, order sentences to create longer sentences
- Together think of words that rhyme with rink.
    - blink, drink, link, mink, pink, sink, wink, etc.
- Lesson 51 worksheet
    - They will use the clues to fill in the blanks. Every answer is an INK word.
    - They will use the words to write a sentence. These are longer sentences. Encourage your child to say the sentence out loud while they are figuring it out. Does it sound right?

Lesson 52
- Students will: write ANK words, write a sentence using a vocabulary word
- Together think of words that rhyme with bank.
    - crank, drank, frank, Hank, rank, sank, tank, etc.
- Lesson 52 worksheet
    - At the top of the worksheet they will use the word box to fill in the blanks.
    - Before your child writes a sentence using one of the words, have your child read the example sentences and talk about what the words mean.
        - The smug girl thinks she's better than everyone else.
        - The envious girl is jealous.

Lesson 53
- Students will: identify nouns, identify common and proper nouns, write the plural form of nouns, write a sentence with a vocabulary word
- Ask your child what a noun is and what the difference is between common and proper nouns.
    - A noun is a person, place, thing, or idea (such as feelings like love and hate).
    - A proper noun is the name of such a noun.
- Ask your child what's the regular way you make a noun plural: one bike, two bikes.
    - Just add an S.
- Lesson 53 worksheet
    - They will underline the nouns in the first part.
    - Then they will label the nouns as P (proper) or C (common).
    - In the next part they will make the words plural. They are all regular plurals.
    - Finally, they will write a sentence using one of the words given. Read the example sentences with your child and talk about what the words mean.
        - Amble means to walk in a relaxed way, enjoying yourself.
        - Hastily means to do something in a real hurry.

Lesson 54
- Students will: write "ANG" words, write a sentence using a vocabulary word
- Together think of words that rhyme with bang.
  - sang, rang, fang, etc.
- Lesson 54 worksheet
  - They will use the words in the word box to fill in the blanks.
  - continued on the next page…
  - The sentences tell a story, and they will label the pictures to show the order of the story.
  - Finally, they will write a sentence using one of the words given.
    - Indignant means being upset that you think you've been treated unfairly.
    - Scornfully means acting like something is worthless.

Lesson 55 (blue and orange crayons)
- Students will: recognize words with the "ONG" phonics pattern, write a sentence with a vocabulary word
- Together think of words that rhyme with song.
  - bong, gong, pong, wrong, etc.
- Lesson 55 worksheet
  - They will color in the "ONG" words orange.
  - Before they write a sentence using one of the words, go over the examples and talk about what the words mean.
    - Anxious means nervous.
    - Feeble means weak.

Lesson 56
- Students will: write "UNG" words, write a sentence using a vocabulary word
- Together think of words that rhyme with sung.
  - rung, stung, hung, etc.
- Lesson 56 worksheet
  - They will fill in the blanks with UNG words.
  - They are asked to write three sentences. They can write about what the girl needs next.

Lesson 57
- Students will: write words with the "DGE" spelling pattern, write a sentence beginning with a capital letter and ending with punctuation
- Together think of words that rhyme with budge.
  - fudge, Mudge, nudge
- Lesson 57 worksheet
  - Look at the DGE at the top of the page. Ask your child what sound those letters make together. They can read the words in the box if they aren't sure.
  - They can write any sentence in the blank. Make sure it begins with a capital letter and ends with a punctuation mark.

Lesson 58 (scissors)
- Students will: identify homonyms
- Ask your child to think of two means of the words hi, ate, and plane.
    - hi, high
    - ate, eight
    - plane, plain
- These are homonyms, words that sound the same but are spelled differently.
- Lesson 58 worksheet
    - They will choose the correct homonym.
    - In the second part they will have to spot the incorrect homonym in the sentence. You could talk together about the two different words and what they each mean.

Lesson 59
- Students will: spell words ending with Y
- Lesson 59 worksheet
    - With your child figure out what words the pictures represent. They all end in Y with an E sound.
        - baby, pony, candy, fifty, money
    - They will need to unscramble the words. Each one is one of the words represented by those pictures.

Lesson 60
- Students will: write words that end in LE
- Lesson 60 worksheet
    - They will have to write words that end in LE without a word box this time. There are pictures as clues to the words.
    - Then there is space to write a sentence, a question. Make sure they begin their sentence with a capital letter and end with a question mark.

Lesson 61 (red and gray crayons)
- Students will: identify the short E sound and the long A sound in words with the EA spelling pattern
- Lesson 61 worksheet
    - Encourage your child to read the words out loud to see which sound they make.

Lesson 62 (scissors, glue)
- Students will: identify the vowel sounds made by the OU spelling pattern
- Lesson 62 worksheet
    - Encourage your child to read the first basket word out loud and then the balloon words to listen for which words have the same sound.

Lesson 63
- Students will: form the plural of regular and irregular nouns
- Lesson 63 worksheet
  - Read over the plural rules together.
  - Encourage your child to use them to complete the worksheet.

Lesson 64
- Students will: write words with the OO spelling pattern that have the vowel sound in the word wood
- Together think of words that rhyme with book.
  - cook, look, took, nook, hook, rook, etc.
- Lesson 64 worksheet
  - Make sure your child knows how to fill in the crossword puzzle.

Lesson 65
- Students will: write a sentence, complete words using the digraphs PH and GH
- Lesson 65 worksheet
  - There is a sentence to copy. Make sure they are starting and ending properly (capital and punctuation).
  - Show your child the GH and PH and tell your child that they can have the F sound. (GH is sometimes silent as in dough.)
  - Each word matches one of the pictures.

Lesson 66
- Students will: identify silent letters in words
- Show your child these words and ask your child to find the letter that is silent, that's not heard when you say the word.

writing   lamb   pile   knit

- Below are the answers.
  - w, b, e, k
  - The ING make the "ing" sound. Each letter is part of that sound.
- Lesson 66 worksheet
  - They will identify which words have a silent letter, find the silent letter, find those words in the picture, and copy those words on the lines provided.

Lesson 67
- Students will: write words with the OI spelling pattern
- Lesson 67 worksheet
  - Have your child read the word list, and ask them what sound the OI makes.
    - oy

Lesson 68
- Students will: write a create sentence using spelling words.
- Lesson 68 worksheet
  - They will use the word list from Lesson 67 to put at least two words into a sentence. There are examples on the page that you could read together.

Lesson 69 (colored pencils is optional)
- Students will: practice parts of speech, copy a sentence, practice capitalizing names
- Lesson 69 worksheet
  - There is a sentence to copy and a fun drawing activity.

Lesson 70 (crayon optional)
- Students will: identify action verbs
- Tell your child that a verb can be an action word. Together think about all the actions going on right now.
  - Some examples…You are sitting. You are talking. You are thinking. The lights are shining. The refrigerator is running. Your stomach is growling. Your eyes are seeing and looking. Your hands are touching.
- Lesson 70 worksheet
  - They will color in the apples that have a verb in them.

Lesson 71
- Students will: practice spelling
- Lesson 71 worksheet
  - They will unscramble the words using the pictures as clues. The pictures don't line up with the words, but each word has a picture clue there.

Lesson 72
- Students will: write a proper sentence, identify verbs
- Ask your child to name some action verbs.
  - run, kick, talk, bounce, ride, sleep, etc.
- Lesson 72 worksheet
  - Have your child read the sentence out loud. It's spoken in a dialect. Can they figure out what it is saying?
    - I have more important things to worry about.
    - They will have to write that out instead of copying it directly.
  - At the bottom of the page they need to find the verbs.

Lesson 73
- Students will: copy a sentence, write regular and irregular plurals
- Lesson 73 worksheet
  - They will copy the sentence being careful to capitalize the name and then they will write the plurals.
    - If they need help, they can turn back to the Lesson 30 page in their workbook, which lists plural rules.

Lesson 74
- Students will: identify verbs
- Lesson 74 worksheet
    - They just need to find the one verb on each line.

Lesson 75
- Students will: write a description
- Talk with your child about their last birthday or their wishes for an upcoming birthday.
- Lesson 75 worksheet
    - They will write about their birthday, the things you were just talking about.
    - If it's physically hard for your child to write, you could write as they dictate to you.

Lesson 76
- Students will: write a description
- Ask your child about their favorite thing to do and why they like it so much.
- Lesson 76 worksheet
    - They will write about their favorite thing and why they like it.
    - Again, if it's physically hard for your child to write, you could write as they dictate to you.

Lesson 77 (crayon optional)
- Students will: identify verbs
- Take turns playing charades with your child.
    - Act out an action verb and guess each other's words.
- Lesson 77 worksheet
    - They can color in the fish with a verb.

Lesson 78
- Students will: identify subjects, action and linking verbs.
- Introduce your child to the other type of verb, a linking verb. These are the types of verbs that tell what someone is.
    - Read the list emphasizing the linking verb.
        - I <u>am</u> tired.
        - He <u>is</u> funny.
        - They <u>are</u> ready.
        - She <u>was</u> persistent.
        - We <u>were</u> prepared.
    - Read the list again and ask your child to name the linking verb in each sentence.
    - Then go through and have your child find the subject of each sentence, who the sentence is about.

- Lesson 78 worksheet
  - They will find the subject and verb of each sentence and then identify verbs as either action verbs or linking verbs.

Lesson 79
- Students will: identify action and linking verbs
- Lesson 79 worksheet
  - They need to find all of the verbs in a sentence. Some sentences have two.

Lesson 80
- Students will: write a creative story
- Lesson 80 worksheet
  - There is a story starter on the page about a skunk.
  - Your child could type this story and you could save it.

Lesson 81
- Students will: write a creative story
- Ask your child what they would do if they were invisible.
- Lesson 81 worksheet
  - They are going to write their invisible adventures as a story.
  - They could also type it or you could write as they dictate if writing it out is hard for them.

Lesson 82 (orange and gray crayons)
- Students will: identify action verbs
- Lesson 82 worksheet
  - They will color in the action verb shapes to make a picture.

Lesson 83 (10 slips of paper)
- Students will: identify action verbs
- Lesson 83 worksheet
  - They will find the action verb in each sentence.
  - Then you can play verb charades together.
    - Here are some ideas: snorkeling, climbing, diving, cheering, worrying, snoring, etc.

Lesson 84
- Students will: correctly use linking verbs
- Lesson 84 worksheet
  - Look at the top of the page together.
  - They will use those words to fill in the blanks.
    - Encourage your child to read the sentence out loud with the word in the blank to listen if it sounds correct.

Lesson 85
- Students will: use question marks and exclamation points in sentences, identify linking verbs
- Lesson 85 worksheet
  - They are to write a question and an answer that ends with an exclamation point, such as, Of course, not!
  - Then they can color or circle the flowers with linking verbs.

Lesson 86
- Students will: identify the parts of a sentence, write a sentence
- Review sentences.
  - A sentence has a capital letter at the beginning, an end mark (like a period), a subject (the noun that the sentence is about) and a predicate (the verb that tells what the noun is doing).
  - Together, look at this sentence.

Mark is coming home today!

  - What is the capital letter at the beginning?
  - What is the end mark?
  - What is the subject? (the noun that the sentence is about)
  - What is the predicate? (the verb that tells what the noun is doing)
    - answers: M, !, Mark, coming
- Lesson 86 worksheet
  - They will put the words in order to make a sentence and then add on their own sentence.
  - Then they will find the simple subject and simple predicate in each sentence.
  - There's space to draw a picture of their story if they like.

Lesson 87
- Students will: write sentences, identify parts of a sentence
- Lesson 87 worksheet:
  - They will rewrite the sentence by putting the words in the correct order.
  - Then they will add two more sentences.
  - Finally, they will find the simple subjects and predicates.

Lesson 88
- Students will: write sentences, identify parts of a sentence
- Lesson 88 worksheet:
  - They will rewrite the sentence by putting the words in the correct order.
  - Then they will add at least two more sentences.
  - Finally, they will find the simple subjects and predicates.

Lesson 89
- Students will: write sentences, identify parts of a sentence
- Lesson 89 worksheet:
    - They will rewrite the sentence by putting the words in the correct order.
    - Then they will add at least two more sentences.
    - Finally, they will find the simple subjects and predicates.

Lesson 90
- Students will: write sentences, identify parts of a sentence
- Lesson 90 worksheet:
    - They will rewrite the sentence by putting the words in the correct order.
    - Then they will add at least two more sentences.
    - Finally, they will find the simple subjects and predicates.

Lesson 91
- Students will: practice spelling words with the OI phonics pattern
- Lesson 91 worksheet
    - Have your child read the list of words out loud.
    - After they are done with their word search, you can give your child a spelling test.
        - Here are the words:
        - oil, boil, coin, join, coil, soil, joint, point, foil, toil, boing, noise

Lesson 92
- Students will: identify more complex linking verbs, write sentences using linking verbs
- Introduce your child to a trick to identify linking verbs.
    - If you can replace it with an =, then it's a linking verb.
    - I am happy. I = happy
    - I feel sad. I = sad
    - This watermelon is juicy. watermelon = juicy
    - This watermelon tastes sweet. watermelon = sweet
- Feel and taste can be action verbs as well.
    - I feel his soft fur. I doesn't equal soft fur.
    - I taste the sour apple in there. I doesn't equal sour apple.
- Lesson 92 worksheet
    - They will find the linking verbs.
    - Then they will write their own sentences with linking verbs.

Lesson 93
- Students will: identify linking verbs, write sentences using linking verbs
- Ask your child if look is an action verb or a linking verb in these sentences.
    - He looks for his book. action, He does not equal book.
    - He looks hungry. linking verb, he = hungry

- Lesson 93 worksheet
  - They will find the linking verb in each sentence but there is one sentence with an action verb they need to be on the lookout for.
  - Then they will write their own two sentences.

Lesson 94 (a book your child is reading)
- Students will: identify linking and action verbs
- Lesson 94 worksheet
  - They will find five linking verbs and five action verbs in a book they are reading.

Lesson 95
- Students will: order directions, use transitional words
- Lesson 95 worksheet
  - Encourage your child to read through all of the steps before beginning.

Lesson 96
- Students will: spell words with the aw spelling pattern
- Lesson 96 worksheet
  - They will do the word search, and then you need to give your child a spelling test.
    - Here are the words:
    - paw, claw, flaw, jaw, paw, draw, law, yawn, lawn, pawn, drawn, straw

Lesson 97 (scissors)
- Students will: identify the proper use of future and past tense, copy a sentence and learn about descriptive writing
- Lesson 97 worksheet
  - There are cards to cut out to match, playing a concentration/memory style game.
    - Encourage your child to read the sentences out loud when they think they have a match.
  - There's a sentence to copy. Read that section with your child and talk about what image the sentence makes them picture and if that's more descriptive than just saying she looked pretty.

Lesson 98
- Students will: make words past tense
- Review with your child consonants and vowels (A E I O U). They will need to know the distinction to follow the spelling rules.

- Lesson 98 worksheet
    - o I think the best way to do this is to use the workbook page. Read each rule and look at any examples and then have your child work on it in front of you, at least the first two sections.
        - ▪ This is all the same as making words plural except for D instead of S.

Lesson 99
- Students will: make complete sentences
- Lesson 99 worksheet
    - o They will write complete sentences by using the words given. Make sure they start with a capital letter and end with a period.
    - o In the second part they will choose what completes the sentence. Does it need a subject? Does it need a verb?

Lesson 100
- Students will: write an ordered story
- Lesson 100 worksheet
    - o There are directions on the page to use the words first, next, last.
        - ▪ You can talk about what they could write about. If they are stumped, help them order something they recently did. They went somewhere, did something, came home.
        - ▪ If they write more than three sentences give your child a high five and/or hug!

Lesson 101
- Students will: write ER words, copy a sentence
- Lesson 101 worksheet
    - o They will copy the sentence at the top of the page paying attention to the details.
    - o They will find the words in the puzzle and then take a spelling test.
        - ▪ Here are the words:
        - ▪ her, verb, silver, sister, stern, fern, herb, herd, mister, blister, mother, father

Lesson 102
- Students will: identify action verbs
- Ask your child what is an action verb.
    - o It's the action the subject is doing.
    - o It doesn't have to be moving around. It can be still "action" like thinking or sleeping.
- Lesson 102 worksheet
    - o They will write the action verb in the sentence.
    - o They will identify the action verb.

Lesson 103
- Students will: identify linking verbs
- Ask your child what is a linking verb.
  - Linking verbs are words that show being. They can be replaced with equals in a sentence.
  - It doesn't have to be moving around. It can be still "action" like thinking or sleeping.
- Lesson 103 worksheet
  - They will write the linking verb in the sentence.
  - They will identify the linking verb.

Lesson 104
- Students will: choose the correct verb tense, identify verbs in the past, present, and future tenses
- Lesson 104 worksheet
  - Read over the top of the worksheet with your child. Go over the past, present, and future by reading the examples.
    - Past tells what happened before.
    - Present tells what's happening now.
    - Future tells what's going to happen.

Lesson 105
- Students will: write sentences using action verbs
- Lesson 105 worksheet
  - They will write three different action verbs.
  - They will write three sentences using those verbs.

Lesson 106
- Students will: identify incorrectly spelled words
- Lesson 106 worksheet
  - They will find which words are spelled incorrectly. Have them read the words out loud to help them decide. There is only one word spelled incorrectly on each line.

Lesson 107
- Students will: write the correct form of verbs, past, present and future
- Ask your child when you use past tense verbs.
  - to tell things that happened in the past
- Ask your child when you use present tense verbs.
  - to tell things happening now
- Ask your child when you use future tense verbs.
  - to tell things that will happen in the future
- Lesson 107 worksheet
  - They will have to write the words on their own.

Lesson 108
- Students will: copy a sentence, identify the subject and predicate of sentences
- Ask your child. What is the subject of the sentence: The dog ate his food.
  - The dog is the subject. The subject of a sentence is what the sentence is about.
- The predicate of a sentence is what the subject does, what it is, or just that it exists.
- Lesson 108 worksheet
  - They will copy the sentence.
  - Then they need to pick out the subject and predicate of the sentences.

Lesson 109
- Students will: identify the complete predicate
- Ask your child what the subject and predicate is.
  - The subject is the noun, the person or thing the sentence is about.
  - The predicate is the verb, what the subject does or is.
- Ask your child to find the subject and predicate in the sentence: The blue toy was my favorite present.
  - The simple subject is toy. The complete subject is the blue toy.
  - The simple predicate is was. The complete predicate is was my favorite present.
- Today they will be finding the complete predicate. It's everything in the sentence that's not part of the subject.
  - Have your child find the complete predicate in the sentence: My little sister gets her curly hair from our dad.
    - gets her curly hair from our dad
    - That's everything that isn't part of the subject. The subject is my little sister.
- Lesson 109 worksheet
  - They will underline the complete predicate.

Lesson 110
- Students will: write a creative story
- The writing prompt is about a ruler, a tyrant, who made a law that everyone had to bow down to his hat. Ask your child what laws they would make if they were king/queen over a land.
- Lesson 110 worksheet
  - They are to write those down on their page. They could type it or you could write for them if the physical part of writing is hard.

Lesson 111
- Students will: practice spelling
- Lesson 111
  - They just need to copy the words.

Lesson 112
- Students will: practice quotation, punctuation, and capitalization; identify linking verbs
- Lesson 112 worksheet
  - They need to copy a sentence. There are two capital letters. They need to pay attention to the punctuation as well. The lines are quotation marks. All the words inside of them are what someone is saying.
  - They need to find the linking verbs.

Lesson 113
- Students will: correct punctuation and capitalization in sentences, practice punctuation and capitalization
- Ask your child what words need to be capitalized.
  - the first letter in a sentence
  - any name: name of a person, name of a place, name of a thing
- Ask your child what types of punctuation go at the end of a sentence.
  - period, exclamation point, question mark
- Lesson 113 worksheet
  - They will find which words should be capitalized and underline them.
  - They will write in the end punctuation.
  - There is also a sentence to copy. They should be careful to copy the commas.

Lesson 114
- Students will: understand and write contractions and their meanings
- Ask your child how they would say I am hungry in a shorter way, with a contraction.
  - I'm hungry.
- Ask your child what you'll in you'll be finished soon means.
  - you will
- Words like could've and hadn't are contractions. They combine two words into one with an apostrophe.
- Lesson 114 worksheet
  - First they just need to pick the correct meaning.
  - Then they have to write the correct meaning.
  - Finally, they have to write the contraction.
    - If they are having any trouble on the second and third parts, encourage them to look above and use those as examples.

Lesson 115
- Students will: write a creative story
- Ask your child what would happen if they ran into a lion on the street. Where do they think it came from? How do they think it would act? Would they ask to take it home as a pet?

- Lesson 115 worksheet
  - They will write a creative story. The story prompt is about running into a lion. If they have another idea, let them go for it.

Lesson 116
- Students will: practice spelling
- Lesson 116 worksheet
  - They just need to copy the words. Encourage them to pay attention!

Lesson 117
- Students will: practice capitalization and punctuation through copywork, identify action words
- Lesson 117 worksheet
  - They will copy the sentence and find the action verbs.

Lesson 118
- Students will: practice capitalization
- Ask your child what words are capitalized in sentences.
  - the first word of each sentence
  - names of people, names of places, names of things
    - Come up with examples together.
      - Oliver, Africa, Legos (for instance)
- Lesson 118 worksheet
  - They will have to show which letters should be capitalized and add in the missing punctuation at the end of each sentence.
  - There's one sentence they will have to rewrite correctly.

Lesson 119
- Students will: sequence a story and complete the story with transition words
- Lesson 119 worksheet
  - They will order the story and fill in the transition words.
  - Have them read the completed story to you.

Lesson 120
- Students will: use transition words to sequence a story
- Lesson 120 worksheet
  - They will order the story and fill in the transition words.
  - Have them read the completed story to you.

Lesson 121
- Students will: practice spelling
- Lesson 121 worksheet
  - They need to copy the words on the page.
  - Encourage your child to pay attention.

Lesson 122
- Students will: identify correct possessive nouns
- Ask your child how you would say the bike of Mike a better way. How do you say the bike belongs to Mike? If your child can't figure it out, use their name and give an example.
  - Mike's bike
- Lesson 122 worksheet
  - Read over the examples on the page together.
  - They just have to pick the correct one. They are all singular nouns followed by an apostrophe S.

Lesson 123
- Students will: identify and write singular possessive nouns
- Lesson 123 worksheet
  - Just like Lesson 122 they will identify the correct possessive nouns.
  - Then they will have to write their own possessives using the names of people in your family. You can help them spell family names.

Lesson 124
- Students will: identify plural possessive nouns
- Ask your child how you show when you are writing that something belongs to someone or something else. When a noun is possessive, how do you show it?
  - with an apostrophe and an S
- If a noun already has an S on the end, all you need to do is add an apostrophe. The S is already there.
- Lesson 124 worksheet
  - They will identify the plural possessive noun.
  - The last one is the name James.
  - There's a phrase to copy with capital letters and a possessive.

Lesson 125
- Students will: determine between its and it's
- Ask your child what words use apostrophes.
  - We've learned about contractions and we've learned about possessive, when something belongs to someone.
- There's a special problem with the word it's, I – T – apostrophe – S. We use it as a contraction, not as possession.
  - What does it's mean, as in: it's in here?
    - it is
- When there is no apostrophe, it means something belongs to it, as in its fur.
- Lesson 125 worksheet
  - Read over the directions together.
  - First, they will choose between its and it's and then write a sentence using each.

Lesson 126
- Students will: practice spelling
- Lesson 126 worksheet
  - They will copy the words.

Lesson 127
- Students will: determine between its and it's
- Review its and it's.
  - What does it's mean, as in: It's already Friday.
    - it is
- When there is no apostrophe, it means something belongs to it, as in its claws.
- Ask your child to try to come up with their own examples of each kind.
- Lesson 127 worksheet
  - First, they will choose between its and it's and then write a sentence using each.

Lesson 128
- Students will: practice editing for capitalization, punctuation, spelling, and word choice
- Lesson 128 worksheet
  - They will have to rewrite the sentences correctly. If writing is physically hard, just have them rewrite the parts needing correcting.

Lesson 129
- Students will: write present and past tense verbs
- Today they will have to write present tense verbs, past tense verbs, and ING verbs.
- Go over the types of verbs they will need. Together come up with examples.
  - ing verb
    - singING, jumpING, readING
  - past tense means happened in the past
    - sang, climbed, closed, drew, wrote, called
  - present tense means that it happens now, in the present
    - read, write, sing, laugh, try, fly, swim
  - action verbs
    - run, jump, slide, crawl, think, sleep, etc…
- Lesson 129 worksheet
  - This is like a Mad Libs activity. They will write the types of verbs listed and then read them in the story. They should choose action verbs.
  - It would be fun to read their story aloud to them.

Lesson 130
- Students will: write present and past tense verbs
- Lesson 130 worksheet
    - This is the same type of activity as in Lesson 129. They will write the types of verbs and choose action verbs.
    - You can ask your child if they need a reminder about the verb types.
    - It would be fun to read their story aloud to them.

Lesson 131
- Students will: practice spelling
- Lesson 131 worksheet
    - They just need to copy the words. Encourage them to pay attention.

Lesson 132
- Students will: begin writing a creative story
- Every sentence needs a subject and predicate. There are examples on the page.
- Lesson 132 worksheet
    - They just need to write one sentence today.

Lesson 133
- Students will: continue writing their creative story
- They will write a sentence with an apostrophe. There are examples on the page.
- Lesson 133 worksheet
    - Read the examples on the page.
    - They will add a sentence to their story where something will belong to someone else.

Lesson 134
- Students will: continue writing their creative story
- They will write a sentence carrying on their story.
- Lesson 134
    - They will add a sentence to their story.

Lesson 135
- Students will: write a compound sentence
- To make a sentence longer you can place a comma and then add a conjunction, a word like and, or, but. There are examples on the page.
- Lesson 135
    - Read the examples on the page.
    - They will continue the last sentence on Lesson 134. They will change the ending punctuation mark into a comma and then add a conjunction before adding their final sentence.

Lesson 136
- Students will: practice spelling
- Lesson 136 worksheet
  - They should look at the word, cover it, write the word, and then check and correct the spelling if need be.

Lesson 137
- Students will: use subject pronouns
- Today they will write in subject pronouns. Pronouns are the words we use to replace nouns in sentences. Use your child's name and tell them a sentence: (NAME) loves to (WHATEVER).
  - The point is to get them to replace their name with the pronoun I.
- Try some more sentences.
  - (MOM) loves (YOUR CHILD'S NAME)
    - They should replace MOM with YOU.
  - (DAD, YOU, and I) love each other.
    - They should use the word WE.
- Lesson 137 worksheet
  - They will fill in the blanks with subject pronouns. They are listed at the top of the page.

Lesson 138
- Students will: use object pronouns
- Today they will write in object pronouns. Pronouns are the words we use to replace nouns in sentences. Use your child's name and tell them a sentence: Please give it to (NAME).
  - The point is to get them to replace their name with the pronoun me.
- Try some more sentences.
  - I will give it to (MOM).
    - They should replace MOM with YOU.
  - Come with MOM, DAD, and I.
    - They should use the word US.
- Lesson 138 worksheet
  - They will fill in the blanks with object pronouns. They are listed at the top of the page.

Lesson 139
- Students will: use object and subject pronouns
- Lesson 139 worksheet
  - They need to choose between object and subject pronouns.
  - The easiest way to do this is to read the sentence out loud to listen for what sounds correct.

Lesson 140
- Students will: write a short story
- There are directions on the page. They will need to use a name, replace it with a pronoun, and use an apostrophe.
- Lesson 140 worksheet
  - Read through the directions together. You can talk through ideas for their story together, but make sure you don't write it for them!

Lesson 141
- Students will: practice phonics using word parts
- Lesson 141 worksheet
  - There's a "word" box at the top of the page that they will use to fill in the blanks.
  - They can try the different word parts in the blanks and read them out loud to listen if they make sense.
  - Then they will write out the complete words.

Lesson 142
- Students will: review contractions
- Lesson 142 worksheet
  - They will match the contractions with what they are short for.
  - Then they are to write the contractions out.

Lesson 143
- Students will: practice vocabulary and spelling
- Lesson 143 worksheet
  - They will match the words to their definitions and copy them onto the lines on the page.

Lesson 144 (red, blue, and green crayons for coloring)
- Students will: identify nouns, pronouns, and verbs; write sentences using nouns, verbs, and pronouns
- Ask your child what are nouns, verbs, and pronouns.
  - people, places, things (officers, Europe, books)
  - actions or show states of being (is, am, seems)
  - replace nouns in sentences (I, you, him, they, us)
- Lesson 144 worksheet
  - They will need to carefully read the directions to show which words are which.
  - Then they will need to write a sentence and then rewrite it with a pronoun, or more!
    - You can reward using more than one pronoun with a high five and/or hug!

Lesson 145
- Students will: write a creative story
- Daydream together about a vacation to a mountain home (or living there). Is it summer or winter? What would you do there? What would happen?
- Lesson 145 worksheet
  - They are to write a story using the writing prompt about staying at a mountain home.
  - You can type it or write it for your child if the writing is hard for them.

Lesson 146
- Students will: identify phonetic blends at the begin and end of words
- Lesson 146 worksheet
  - They will use the pictures to figure out what word they are trying to find the sounds for. They could be the first two or the last two letters of the word.
  - At the bottom of the page there are words to write and then they are to write their own three words that end with CK.

Lesson 147
- Students will: identify and write contractions
- Lesson 147 worksheet
  - They just need to match the contractions with their meanings.
  - At the bottom of the page there are lines to write the contractions listed and two of their choosing. They can use the page to help them.

Lesson 148
- Students will: use base words and suffixes to identify word meanings
- Lesson 148 worksheet
  - They will write the words next to their meanings.
  - Go over the worksheet with them after they are done and have them find similar suffixes and what's common in their definitions.

Lesson 149
- Students will: practice phonics using word parts
- Lesson 149 worksheet
  - There's a "word" box at the top of the page that they will use to fill in the blanks.
  - They can try the different word parts in the blanks and read them out loud to listen if they make sense.
  - Then they will write out the complete words.

Lesson 150
- Students will: write a creative story using an adverb and words with suffixes
- Lesson 150 worksheet
  - They need to write at least four sentences.
  - The story starter is simply: He/She bravely…

Lesson 151
- Students will: practice vocabulary and spelling
- Lesson 151 worksheet
  - They will match the words to their definitions and copy them onto the lines on the page.

Lesson 152
- Students will: identify contractions, pronouns, common nouns
- Lesson 152 worksheet
  - They will copy the sentence on the page and then identify the parts of the sentence.

Lesson 153
- Students will: identify contractions, pronouns, proper nouns
- Lesson 153 worksheet
  - They will copy the sentence on the page and then identify the parts of the sentence.

Lesson 154
- Students will: identify contractions, pronouns, proper nouns
- Lesson 154 worksheet
  - They will copy the sentence on the page and then identify the parts of the sentence.

Lesson 155
- Students will: write three sentences using quotation marks and contractions
- Lesson 155 worksheet
  - They will write sentences in the format of the ones they've been copying over the last few days.

Lesson 156
- Students will: copy a sentence
- Lesson 156 worksheet
  - They just need to copy the sentence. There is a space to draw a picture of it to show they understand what the sentence is saying.

Lesson 157
- Students will: practice phonics using word parts
- Lesson 157 worksheet
  - There's a "word" box at the top of the page that they will use to fill in the blanks.
  - They can try the different word parts in the blanks and read them out loud to listen if they make sense.
  - Then they will write out the complete words.

Lesson 158
- Students will: practice vocabulary and spelling
- Lesson 158 worksheet
    - They will match the words to their definitions and copy them onto the lines on the page.

Lesson 159
- Students will: identify plural nouns, past and present tense verbs
- Lesson 159 worksheet
    - They will copy the sentence on the page and then identify the parts of the sentence.

Lesson 160
- Students will: write a descriptive story
- Lesson 160 worksheet
    - Read the top of the page together and listen to your child's ideas.

Lesson 161
- Students will: identify vowel sounds made by vowel pairs
- Lesson 161 worksheet
    - Encourage your child to try the different vowel sounds in the blanks to listen for what makes a word.
    - They just need to write the vowels in the blanks.

Lesson 162
- Students will: identify nouns and verbs
- Ask your child what are nouns and verbs.
    - person, place, thing
    - action, word that shows a state of being
- Ask your child about the word park. Is it a noun or a verb?
    - This is a trick question. You can go to a park to play. That's a thing, a noun. Or, you can park your car, something you do, an action, a verb.
    - They will need to pay attention to how words are used in the sentences to identify if they are nouns or verbs.
- Lesson 162 worksheet
    - They are going to identify words that nouns or verbs.
    - There are words in there that are used as nouns and verbs: roll/rolled, swing/swung, shop/shopped, practice/practice. They need to pay attention to tell if they are actions or things.

Lesson 163 (scissors)
- Students will: identify homophones
- Today they are going to work with homophones. They are words that sound the same but are spelled differently from each other. Do they know the difference between them?

- Lesson 163 worksheet
    - They need to cut out the squares and match the words to their definitions. They each have a pair that sounds the same.
    - You could hold onto these cards for review on Lesson 164.

Lesson 164
- Students will: spell homophones
- If you have your homophone squares, let your child look them over. They are going to be spelling those words today.
- Lesson 164 worksheet
    - They will write the words they used in the matching game from Lesson 163.

Lesson 165
- Students will: be evaluated on spelling homophones
- Lesson 165 worksheet
    - Read the sentences to your child and have them spell the homophones.
    - see – I see the blue sky.
    - sea – The sea is salty.
    - deer – A deer came into the yard last night.
    - dear – My family is dear to me.
    - die – The leaves die in the autumn.
    - dye – We used green dye in our project.
    - meet – Can we meet at the park?
    - meat – Vegetarians don't eat meat.
    - road – The road was full of traffic.
    - rode – We rode our bikes all day.

Lesson 166 (library)
- Students will: start a research project
- They will be starting a project today that will last through Lesson 180.
    - They just need to pick a topic today.
    - They can do this in the workbook, but you might decide to work on a computer for this and have it as a typed project with pictures from the internet instead of drawings.
    - You could consider getting books on their topic to do their research instead of relying on the internet.
- Lesson 166 worksheet
    - They just need to write their topic on the page and draw a picture. It can become the cover of a book they are writing on the subject.

Lesson 167
- Students will: research
- Lesson 167 worksheet
    - They need to write at least two facts. They should write it down and write down where they got it from.

Lesson 168
- Students will: research
- Lesson 168 worksheet
  - They need to write at least two facts. They should write it down and write down where they got it from.

Lesson 169
- Students will: research
- Lesson 169 worksheet
  - They need to write at least two facts. They should write it down and write down where they got it from.

Lesson 170
- Students will: write a non-fiction book
- Lesson 170 worksheet
  - They will write one fact on the page and add a picture. There are five pages for facts, so they need to pick their favorite facts.

Lesson 171
- Students will: write a non-fiction book
- Lesson 171 worksheet
  - They will write one fact on the page and add a picture.

Lesson 172
- Students will: write a non-fiction book
- Lesson 172 worksheet
  - They will write one fact on the page and add a picture.

Lesson 173
- Students will: write a non-fiction book
- Lesson 173 worksheet
  - They will write one fact on the page and add a picture.

Lesson 174
- Students will: write a non-fiction book
- Lesson 174 worksheet
  - They will write one fact on the page and add a picture.

Lesson 175
- Students will: write a resource page
- Lesson 175 worksheet
  - They will write their resources all on one page.
  - This is so that it can all be compiled into a book.

Lesson 176
- Students will: write an introduction
- Lesson 176 worksheet
  - They just need to write one sentence telling what they researched about. "I learned about frogs." Just simple.

Lesson 177
- Students will: write a conclusion
- Lesson 177 worksheet
  - They are to tell what they think about their topic. "I think frogs are awesome."

Lesson 178
- Students will: edit and compile a book
- Lesson 178 worksheet
  - You can help take the pages out of the workbook and staple them all together into a book.
  - They can also look over the pages with you and look for anything that's not correct. Did they use capital letters and ending punctuation?
- Maybe your child would like to read their book to someone.

Lesson 179
- Students will: write a paragraph
- Lesson 179 worksheet
  - They are going to copy their book onto one page.
  - They are writing a paragraph: intro, details, conclusion.
    - You could also think about typing it up together.

Lesson 180 (blue and green crayons)
- Students will: review action and linking verbs
- You can ask your child for some examples of linking verbs.
  - am, is, are, was, were, will be, has been, etc.
- Lesson 180 worksheet
  - See if they can do it without a review. There are no tricky linking verbs, like seems.
- Celebrate your child completing second grade language arts!

EP Language Arts 2

Workbook Answers

Lesson 1

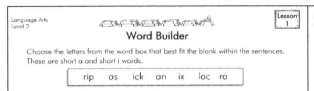

Word Builder

Choose the letters from the word box that best fit the blank within the sentences. These are short a and short i words.

| rip | as | ick | an | ix | lac | ra |

Our v **an** broke down yesterday.

My dog plays fetch with a st **ick** .

We had a bl **as** t at our block party.

I m **ix** ed up a batch of cookie dough.

My favorite dog is a b **lac** k lab.

We'd love to go to Europe on a t **rip** one day.

I had to g **ra** b a cookie before my brother ate them all.

Lesson 5

Find the Nouns

Color red (circled) the common noun flowers. Color blue (underlined) the proper noun flowers. Names of people, places, and things begin with a capital letter and are proper nouns.

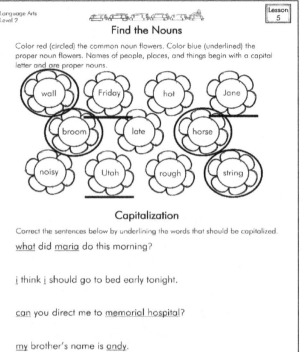

Capitalization

Correct the sentences below by underlining the words that should be capitalized.

what did maria do this morning?

i think i should go to bed early tonight.

can you direct me to memorial hospital?

my brother's name is andy.

i forgot to bring my glasses when we went to ohio.

Lesson 6

Contractions

Use this matching game to help you review some contractions and their meanings. First, read through the words - the contraction is to the right of the words it represents. Then cut out the squares, mix them up, flip them over, and try to match them back again.

would not	wouldn't	will not	won't
you have	you've	could not	couldn't
we are	we're	we have	we've
did not	didn't	I will	I'll
can not	can't	she will	she'll

Lesson 8

Capitalization and Punctuation

Choose the proper way to write each sentence.

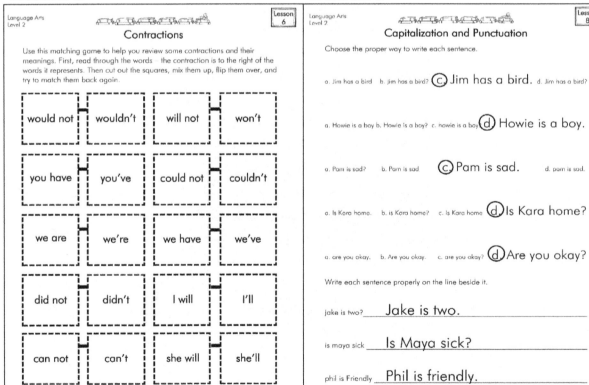

a. Jim has a bird   b. jim has a bird?   (c) Jim has a bird.   d. Jim has a bird?

a. Howie is a boy   b. Howie is a boy?   c. howie is a boy   (d) Howie is a boy.

a. Pam is sad?   b. Pam is sad   (c) Pam is sad.   d. pam is sad.

a. Is Kara home.   b. is Kara home?   c. Is Kara home   (d) Is Kara home?

a. are you okay.   b. Are you okay.   c. are you okay?   (d) Are you okay?

Write each sentence properly on the line beside it.

jake is two?   Jake is two.

is maya sick   Is Maya sick?

phil is Friendly   Phil is friendly.

Lesson 9

Writing

Copy these lines of a poem: *The cat she walks on padded claws.*
The wolf on the hills lays stealthy paws.

The cat she walks on
padded claws.
The wolf on the hills lays
stealthy paws.

Ordering Directions

Put these directions for making a peanut butter and jelly sandwich in order using the words in the box.

| first | second | third | fourth | fifth | then | finally |

__third__ Spread the peanut butter on the bread.

__fourth__ Open the jelly.

__finally__ Enjoy your lunch!

__then__ Put both pieces of bread together.

__fifth__ Spread the jelly on the peanut butter.

__second__ Open the peanut butter.

__first__ Gather the bread, peanut butter, jelly, and knife.

Lesson 10

Correct the Capitalization

Correct the sentences below by underlining the words that should be capitalized. Remember that all sentences must begin with a capital letter. Proper nouns should be capitalized as well. Just do your best and learn from any mistakes!

<u>my</u> favorite holiday is <u>christmas</u>.

<u>my</u> favorite month is <u>december</u>.

<u>my</u> best friend lives on <u>main street</u>.

<u>i</u> like to ride the cable cars in <u>san francisco</u>.

<u>we</u> are going to the zoo on the first <u>friday</u> in <u>april</u>.

<u>she's</u> taking the train to <u>indianapolis</u> next week.

Write the sentences correctly on the lines below them.

i live in the united states.

I live in the United States.

my dad's name is alan.

My dad's name is Alan.

Lesson 11

Compound Words

A **compound word** is one word made out of two words. *Bedroom* is one word, but it's made from the two words *bed* and *room*. Use the words from the box to make compound words out of the words listed.

| cone | stick | muffs | day | place | ground |
| stairs | ball | shine | boy | cut | chair |

birth __day__

cow __boy__

up __stairs__

sun __shine__

fire __place__

hair __cut__

wheel __chair__

play __ground__

snow __ball__

ear __muffs__

pine __cone__

drum __stick__

Lesson 12

Writing

Copy this sentence: *My clothes are soft and warm, fold upon fold, but I'm so sorry for the poor out in the cold.*

My clothes are soft and
warm, fold upon fold, but
I'm so sorry for the poor
out in the cold.

Which two words in the sentence above rhyme?

__fold__   __cold__

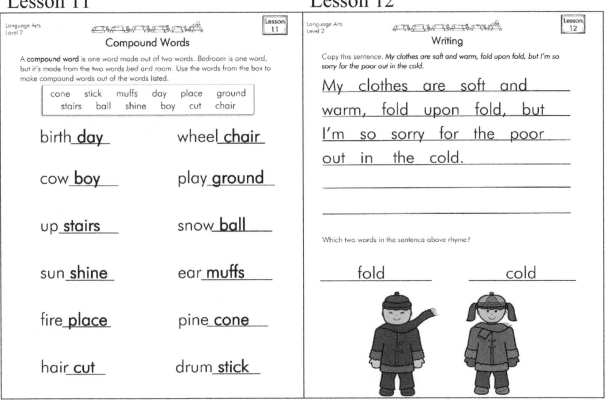

Lesson 13

Writing

Copy these lines of a poem: *If all were sun and never rain, There'd be no rainbow still.*

If all were sun and never rain,
There'd be no rainbow still.

Capitalization and Punctuation

Underline the words in each sentence that need to be capitalized. Then fill in the punctuation mark that best fits each sentence.

i'm so excited for **thanksgiving**!

would you like to go to **central park**?

what is your favorite food from **taco bell**?

help!

what is your favorite **christmas** song?

my november birthday is on a **saturday** this year.

Lesson 14

Writing

Copy this line from a poem by Christina Rossetti: *Stroke a flint, and there is nothing to admire: Strike a flint, and forthwith flash out sparks of fire.*

Stroke a flint, and there is
nothing to admire: Strike a
flint, and forthwith flash out
sparks of fire.

Which two words in the poem above rhyme?

admire   fire

Lesson 18

Plurals

Choose the correct plural form of the words below.

elf
a. elfs   (b.) **elves**

cup
(a.) **cups**   b. cupes

patch
(a.) **patches**   b. patchs

kiss
a. kiss's   (b.) **kisses**

toy
a. toyes   (b.) **toys**

baby
a. babys   (b.) **babies**

wish
(a.) **wishes**   b. wish

fish
a. fishes   (b.) **fish**

Fill in the blank with the plural form of the words below.

color **colors**   box **boxes**

peach **peaches**   play **plays**

miss **misses**   berry **berries**

thief **thieves**   sheep **sheep**

Lesson 19

Rhyming

Circle the rhyming words in this poem by Christina Rossetti. Underline the words that repeat.

*Fly away, fly away over the (sea)
Sun-loving swallow, for summer is (done;)
Come again, come again, come back to (me,)
Bringing the summer and bringing the (sun.)*

Write two poem lines. Start each line with a repeating phrase and rhyme the last words. For instance: *Summer's here, summer's here, let's go and play.*
                                                                                                                                                    Winter's come, winter's come, inside we'll stay.

Make up your own poem or copy the line *Summer's here, summer's here, let's go and play* and then write your own last line. Make sure it rhymes with play!

(answers will vary)

Lesson 20

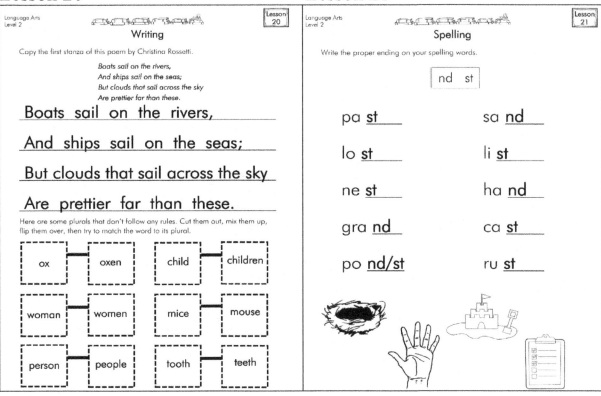

Lesson 21

Spelling

Write the proper ending on your spelling words.

| nd   st |

pa __st__   sa __nd__

lo __st__   li __st__

ne __st__   ha __nd__

gra __nd__   ca __st__

po __nd/st__   ru __st__

Lesson 22

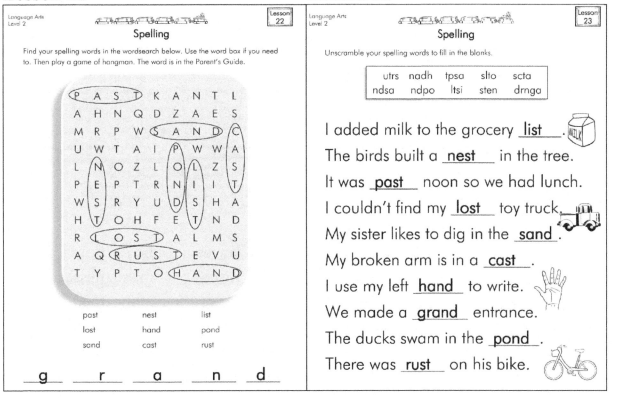

Lesson 23

Spelling

Unscramble your spelling words to fill in the blanks.

| utrs | nadh | tpsa | slto | scta |
| ndsa | ndpo | ltsi | sten | drnga |

I added milk to the grocery __list__ .

The birds built a __nest__ in the tree.

It was __past__ noon so we had lunch.

I couldn't find my __lost__ toy truck.

My sister likes to dig in the __sand__ .

My broken arm is in a __cast__ .

I use my left __hand__ to write.

We made a __grand__ entrance.

The ducks swam in the __pond__ .

There was __rust__ on his bike.

Lesson 24

Spelling

Now try to spell your words. Use the pictures to help you remember the words.

My sister likes to dig in the __sand__ .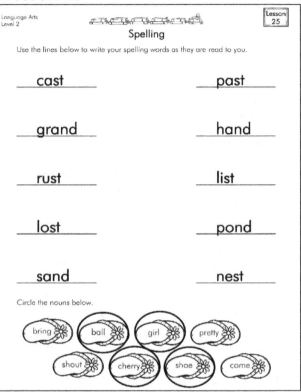

The birds built a __nest__ in the tree.

My dog's broken leg is in a __cast__ .

I added milk to the grocery __list__ .

I use my left __hand__ to write.

Lesson 25

Spelling

Use the lines below to write your spelling words as they are read to you.

cast	past
grand	hand
rust	list
lost	pond
sand	nest

Circle the nouns below.

bring   ball   girl   pretty
shout   cherry   shoe   come

Lesson 28

Singular and Plural nouns

A noun is *singular* when it refers to only one person, place, thing, or idea:

apple   kid   flower   bee

A noun is *plural* when it refers to more than one person, place, thing, or idea:

apples   kids   flowers   bees

The regular plural form of a noun is made by simply adding an **s** to the end of the word. The following list is a mix of singular and plural nouns. If the noun is in the singular form, write its plural form in the blank. If the noun is in the plural form, write its singular form in the blank.

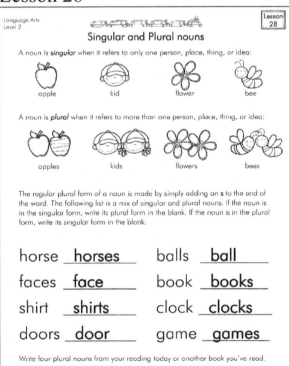

horse	__horses__	balls	__ball__
faces	__face__	book	__books__
shirt	__shirts__	clock	__clocks__
doors	__door__	game	__games__

Write four plural nouns from your reading today or another book you've read.

__(ans wers will vary)__

Lesson 30

Plural Rules

The regular plural of nouns is made by adding an S to the end of the word. But there are exceptions to this rule. We call these exceptions **irregular plurals**.

We make the plural of nouns that end in CH, SH, X, or SS by adding ES.

one dress	one fox	one couch
two dresses	two foxes	two couches

We make the plural of some nouns that end in F or FE by changing the F or FE to V and adding ES.

one leaf	one elf
two leaves	two elves

We make the plural of nouns that end in Y not following a vowel by changing the Y to I and adding ES.

one cherry	one fly
two cherries	two flies

And of course, there are many words that just don't follow a rule.

one woman, two women	one child, two children
one sheep, two sheep	one cactus, two cacti

Write the plurals:

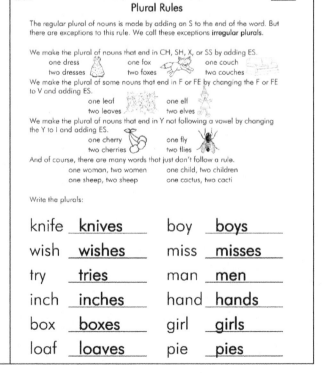

knife	__knives__	boy	__boys__
wish	__wishes__	miss	__misses__
try	__tries__	man	__men__
inch	__inches__	hand	__hands__
box	__boxes__	girl	__girls__
loaf	__loaves__	pie	__pies__

Lesson 35

Fishing for Nouns

A **noun** is a person (Jeffrey, boy, sister), place (post office, church, Chicago), thing (ball, dog, computer), or idea (love, fear, happiness). Circle the fish below that contain nouns.

Lesson 36

Ar words

Fill in the missing "ar" word using the word box below.

arm	dark	yard	far	barn
car	bark	harp	cart	park

I went out into the **y a r d** to play.

We filled our **c a r t** at the store.

My dog likes to **b a r k** at the TV.

The swings at the **p a r k** are fun.

The **h a r p** makes a pretty sound.

My grandmother lives **f a r** away.

The hayloft is in the **b a r n**.

My sister is afraid of the **d a r k**.

His **a r m** was in a sling.

My mom drives a red **c a r**.

Lesson 37

Er sound

Fill in the missing "er" word using the word box below. Then write more "er" words on the blank at the bottom.

serve	skirt	burp	curve	every	blur	turkey	squirrel

The **s q u i r r e l** ran up the tree.

She had flowers on her **s k i r t**.

I **b u r p** when I drink soda.

The sign marked the **c u r v e** in the road.

The **t u r k e y** was delicious.

The cars went so fast they were a **b l u r**.

My mother likes to **s e r v e** us dinner.

I brush my teeth **e v e r y** day.

Lesson 38

Proper Nouns

Proper nouns are names of people, places, things and ideas. Read the story below. Circle the proper nouns and then write them on the lines below the story. Make sure to capitalize them on the lines!

My favorite day of the week is (friday.) I start the day with my favorite cereal, (choco chunkies.) It's a special treat I only get to have on that day. Then I find all of my library books from the previous week. Friday is the day we get to go to (central library) and pick out new books. I love reading and finding new stories! Friday afternoon, we get to have lunch at my favorite sandwich shop, (anderson's deli.) The sandwich I get is called (monster cheese.) It's so warm and toasty and delicious. That evening is basketball practice. This year, my team is called (the crushers) and my dad is the coach. I'm on the team with my best friend (james.) Finally, when I fall into bed after a long day, it's always nice to realize the next day is (saturday,) so I can just relax!

1. Friday
2. Choco Chunkies
3. Central Library
4. Anderson's Deli
5. Monster Cheese
6. The Crushers
7. James
8. Saturday

Lesson 40

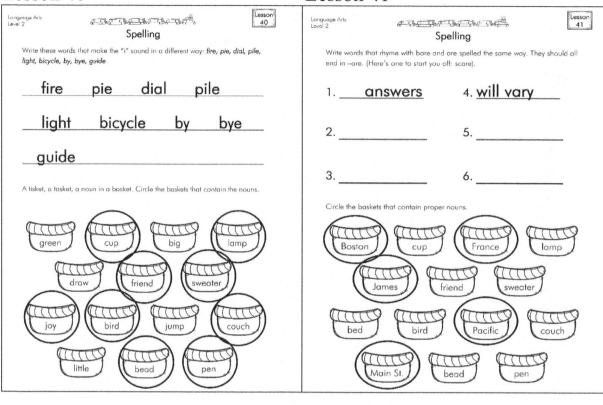

Lesson 40

Spelling

Write these words that make the "i" sound in a different way: *fire, pie, dial, pile, light, bicycle, by, bye, guide.*

fire   pie   dial   pile

light   bicycle   by   bye

guide

A tisket, a tasket, a noun in a basket. Circle the baskets that contain the nouns.

green   cup   big   lamp

draw   friend   sweater

joy   bird   jump   couch

little   bead   pen

Lesson 41

Lesson 41

Spelling

Write words that rhyme with bare and are spelled the same way. They should all end in –are. (Here's one to start you off: scare).

1. **answers**   4. **will vary**

2. _____   5. _____

3. _____   6. _____

Circle the baskets that contain proper nouns.

Boston   cup   France   lamp

James   friend   sweater

bed   bird   Pacific   couch

Main St.   bead   pen

Lesson 42

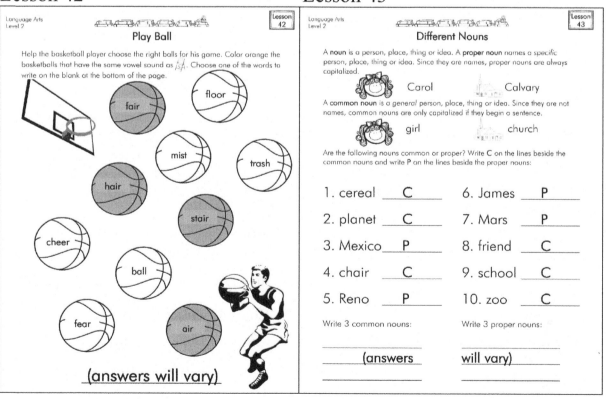

Lesson 42

Play Ball

Help the basketball player choose the right balls for his game. Color orange the basketballs that have the same vowel sound as *air*. Choose one of the words to write on the blank at the bottom of the page.

floor

fair

mist

trash

hair

stair

cheer

ball

fear

air

(answers will vary)

Lesson 43

Lesson 43

Different Nouns

A **noun** is a person, place, thing or idea. A **proper noun** names a specific person, place, thing or idea. Since they are names, proper nouns are always capitalized.

Carol   Calvary

A **common noun** is a general person, place, thing or idea. Since they are not names, common nouns are only capitalized if they begin a sentence.

girl   church

Are the following nouns common or proper? Write C on the lines beside the common nouns and write P on the lines beside the proper nouns:

1. cereal   C   6. James   P

2. planet   C   7. Mars   P

3. Mexico   P   8. friend   C

4. chair   C   9. school   C

5. Reno   P   10. zoo   C

Write 3 common nouns: Write 3 proper nouns:

(answers   will vary)

Lesson 44

Oy!

Find the hidden toy! Color red all of the spaces with words that have the same vowel sound as "toy." Color the rest of the words brown.

mask · run · voice · pest · most · joy · point · plug · step · oink · join · boy · plug · coin · hoist · joint · moist · swing · play · leap · moon

Write your name, phone number, and address:

Name: _____   Phone: _____

Address: _____

Lesson 45

Crossword

Fill in the correct word from the word box to complete the crossword puzzle.

Word box:

clouds	ouch
house	owl
howl	pounce
mouse	proud

Across
1. The _____ was hooting in the trees.
4. The _____ ate all of the cheese.
5. Our dog will sometimes _____ at the door.
6. Some cats love to _____.

Down
1. When I fell off my bike, I screamed, "_____!"
2. Our _____ is the smallest on our street.
3. The sky was full of _____.
6. I am _____ when I work hard.

Circle the common nouns and underline the proper nouns:

cat · Utah · fast · tree · big · Pete · pail · face · eat · brick · Jane · meal · wall · pink · Earth

---

Lesson 46

Aw sound

Use the words from the box to fill in the blanks. Then draw a picture of one of the sentences or draw your own "aw" scene.

saw	paw	cause	draw	pause	flaw

My dog licked his __paw__.

I love to __draw__ pictures.

We had to __pause__ the movie.

My biggest __flaw__ is a lack of patience.

I __saw__ a deer in the backyard.

She's raising money for a good __cause__.

Lesson 47

AL words

Use the words from the box to fill in the blanks. Then find them in the word search. Finally, write 3 words that rhyme with the words from the box.

fall	walked	hall	call	all	tall

I heard my mom __call__ for me so I __walked__ down the __hall__. I tripped over a toy and had quite the __fall__. I needed a bandage for my knee. Thankfully, I am __tall__ because they were on the top shelf. As my little sister would say, the bandage made it __all__ better.

__(ex. ball, mall, talked, wall, etc.)__

Lesson 48

Nouns

Circle the common nouns and underline the proper nouns. Then sort them and write them in the blanks at the bottom.

1. <u>Jessica</u> and <u>Andrew</u> went to <u>Matthew's</u> (house)
2. The (boys) all ran around <u>Northgate Mall</u>.
3. The (girls) played with the (ball) at <u>Griffith Park</u>.
4. <u>Maya</u> loved to dress up her (doll)
5. <u>Kate</u> had some (cake)
6. The (book) belonged to <u>Jack</u>.
7. <u>Henry</u> was <u>Central Zoo's</u> biggest (tortoise)
8. There was a loud (noise) in the (backyard)

Common nouns:

1. __answers will__
2. _____
3. _____
4. _____
5. _____

Proper nouns:

1. __vary__
2. _____
3. _____
4. _____
5. _____

Lesson 49

Story Order

Read the story below. Then put the pictures in the order they happened in the story by numbering the boxes. Finally, underline the 5 words in the story that have the long a sound.

During the week, I do a lot of the **same** things. I **wake** up in the morning and **make** my bed. I have breakfast and then start my school work. I'm usually done by lunch time. After lunch, I love to ride my bike. It's good exercise and a lot of fun. I also like to build things and try to figure out how things work. At the end of a long **day**, I love to relax in the bathtub. What does your **daily** schedule look like?

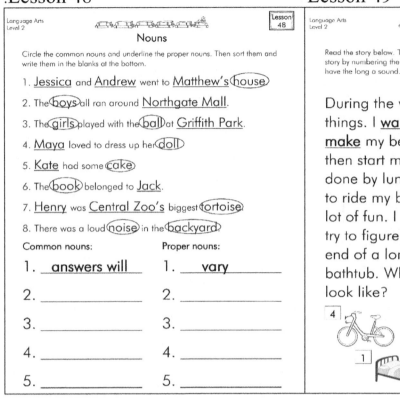

Lesson 50

Ing words

Each of the pictures represents a word that ends in **ing**. Write the word beside the picture it represents. Then write four sentences using ing words.

swing

wing

string

ring

spring

_____
_____

(answers will vary)

_____
_____

Lesson 51

Ink sound

Fill in the blank with the "ink" word that best fits the description.

think	rink	ink	drink	brink	stink	sink
	pink	wink	blink	mink		

What a skunk has	stink
When I close my eyes fast	blink
What's inside a pen	ink
What I do with my brain	think
What I do with milk	drink

Put these sentences in the correct order.

going	park	She	brother.	with	to	her	the	is

<u>She is going to the park with her brother.</u>

coming,	excited!	and	cousin	I'm	is	so	My

<u>My cousin is coming, and I'm so excited!</u>

Lesson 52

Ank sound

Fill in the missing "ank" words below.

| bank | thank | drank | sank | crank | stank | plank | rank |

After the skunk sprayed, the air __stank__ .

I __drank__ some milk.

My heart __sank__ when I heard the news.

I always say please and __thank__ you.

The deck had a loose __plank__ of wood.

We got some money at the __bank__ .

When I __rank__ my favorite colors, red is number one.

The old fashioned ice cream maker had a hand __crank__ .

Write a sentence using **smug** or **envious**. Examples: She thought she was the best swimmer ever and was so **smug** about it. She was **envious** of how well the other girls could swim.

_____

_____

Lesson 53

Noun Review

Underline all the nouns in each sentence.

The <u>girls</u> played with their <u>dolls</u> in the <u>playroom</u>.

The <u>boys</u> kicked the <u>ball</u> in the <u>backyard</u>.

<u>Samuel</u> read a <u>book</u> in his <u>bed</u>.

The <u>phone</u> rang and woke up <u>Jan</u>.

Write **P** for proper or **C** for common in the blank beside each noun.

book	C	James	P
Chicago	P	sock	C
Jupiter	P	love	C

Write the plural of each word in the blank beside it.

finger	fingers	cup	cups
lamp	lamps	picture	pictures
flower	flowers	friend	friends

Write a sentence using **amble** or **hastily**. Examples: He **ambled** down the street whistling a tune. He **hastily** ate breakfast and spilled his juice.

(answers will vary)

_____

Lesson 54

Ang sound

Fill in the blanks with the "ang" word that best fits. Then put the pictures in the order of the story by numbering the boxes.

| sang | rang | bang | hang |

The phone __rang__ and woke me up. It was my Aunt Cathy. She __sang__ Happy Birthday to me. I sat straight up in bed and tried not to __bang__ my head on the wall. I told my aunt, "Don't __hang__ up, but my birthday is next week!" We had a good laugh.

3   1   2

Write a sentence using **indignant** or **scornfully**. Examples: She was **indignant** that someone would step on her foot. She looked at the bread **scornfully** and said, "I would never eat that!"

(answers will vary)

Lesson 55

Ong sound

Color orange all of the words in the puzzle that rhyme with "song." Color the rest of the words blue.

sing   trace   one   plus   wrong   fang   blame   song   right   swung   long   throng   tong   thing   place   bed

Write a sentence using **anxious** or **feeble**. Examples: The big storm made him **anxious**. He has been sick for so long he has become **feeble**.

(answers will vary)

_____

Lesson 56

Ung sound

Fill in the "ung" words that best fit the blanks below. Then write 3 more sentences about what the girl does at home.

sung   rung   hung   swung   flung

A girl **swung** from the monkey bars at the playground. As she **hung** there, she thought of the song they had **sung** in choir about a monkey swinging through the trees. When she climbed down the ladder, her shoe got stuck on a **rung**. "Maybe I wouldn't make a very good monkey," she thought as she **flung** herself down.

_____

_____

_____ **(answers will vary)** _____

_____

Lesson 57

Dge sound

Fill in the "dge" words that best fit the blanks below. One is a proper noun! If you want to, you can color the pictures that correspond to the sentences.

Pledge   edge   badge   fudge   lodge

I earned a **badge** in my scout program.

I love to make peppermint **fudge** with my mom.

We stayed at the **lodge** when we went on vacation.

I saw a rainbow at the **edge** of the clouds.

We said the **Pledge** of Allegiance.

Write a sentence about anything you want. Remember how to start and finish it.

(answers will vary)

_____

Lesson 58

Homonyms

Homonyms are words that sound alike but have different spellings and meanings. For each sentence below, circle the homonym that best fits the sentence. Learn from any mistakes you make.

The ___ was drinking from the stream.　(deer)　dear

I ___ the bus and was late.　(missed)　mist

I really ___ to get more sleep.　knead　(need)

The ___ flew overhead.　(plane)　plain

That's my mom over ___.　their　(there)

The doctor was an ___ late.　our　(hour)

My cat has a fluffy ___.　(tail)　tale

The wrong form of the homonym is in each sentence. Circle the incorrect word and write the correct one on the line: sum, rode, meat, and bear.

The (bare) ate all of the honey.　**bear**

We (road) our bikes all the way home.　**rode**

Carnivores eat (meet).　**meat**

Add the numbers to find the (some).　**sum**

Lesson 59

Word Scramble

Unscramble the letters to make words that end with the same ending as ➡.

tfyif　**fifty**

ydnca　**candy**

npoy　**pony**

byab　**baby**

yenmo　**money**

Write a sentence about anything you want. Remember how to start and finish it.

(answers will vary)

_____

Lesson 60

Le ending

Fill in the "le" words that best fit the blanks below. Use the pictures if you need help figuring out the word. You can color the pictures if you want to.

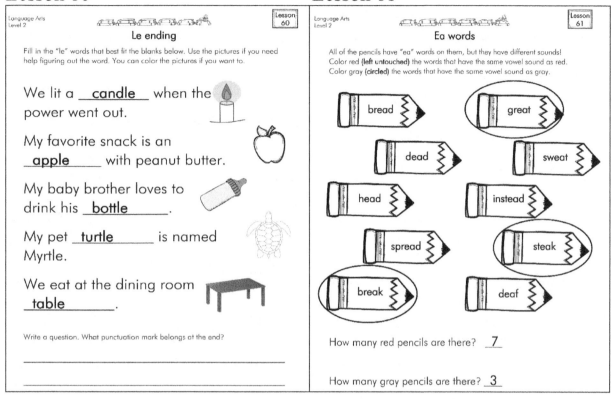

We lit a __candle__ when the power went out.

My favorite snack is an __apple__ with peanut butter.

My baby brother loves to drink his __bottle__ .

My pet __turtle__ is named Myrtle.

We eat at the dining room __table__ .

Write a question. What punctuation mark belongs at the end?

_____

_____

Lesson 61

Ea words

All of the pencils have "ea" words on them, but they have different sounds!
Color red (left untouched) the words that have the same vowel sound as red.
Color gray (circled) the words that have the same vowel sound as gray.

bread

great

dead

sweat

head

instead

spread

steak

break

deaf

How many red pencils are there? __7__

How many gray pencils are there? __3__

Lesson 62

Ou words

Each basket has a word on it. Cut and paste the balloons with the same vowel sound onto the strings coming out of that basket.

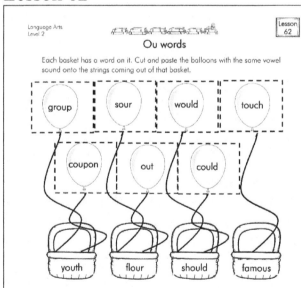

group   sour   would   touch

coupon   out   could

youth   flour   should   famous

Lesson 63

Plural Review

Fill in the plural of each word in the blank beside the word. For many nouns, you simply add an "s" to make it plural. Here are some reminders about the exceptions:

> For nouns that end in ch, sh, x, o, or ss, add "es."
> For some nouns ending in f or fe, change those endings to "ves."
> For nouns that end in a consonant followed by a y, change the y to "ies."
> For some nouns that have oo, change oo to "ee."
> Many other irregular nouns don't follow any rule: children, fish, men, etc.

foot __feet__   toy __toys__

itch __itches__   elf __elves__

baby __babies__   woman __women__

fox __foxes__   ball __balls__

hero __heroes__   deer __deer__

kiss __kisses__   hug __hugs__

goose __geese__   knife __knives__

candy __candies__   box __boxes__

Lesson 64

Plural Review

Use the pictures to fill in the crossword puzzle. All of the words have "oo" in them.

Across:

2.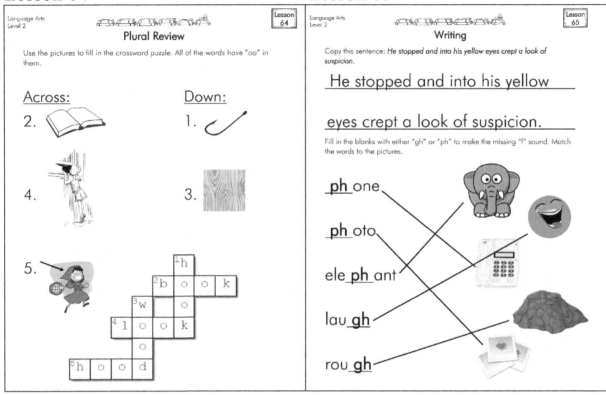

4.

5.

Down:

1.

3.

¹h

²b o o k

³w o

⁴l o o k

o

⁵h o o d

Lesson 65

Writing

Copy this sentence: *He stopped and into his yellow eyes crept a look of suspicion.*

He stopped and into his yellow

eyes crept a look of suspicion.

Fill in the blanks with either "gh" or "ph" to make the missing "f" sound. Match the words to the pictures.

ph one

ph oto

ele **ph** ant

lau **gh**

rou **gh**

Lesson 66

Writing

Underline the silent letters in the words that contain them below. Then find those words in the picture. Finally, write them on the lines at the bottom.

| two | big | kni**f**e | dog | com**b** | sign | wav**e** | man |

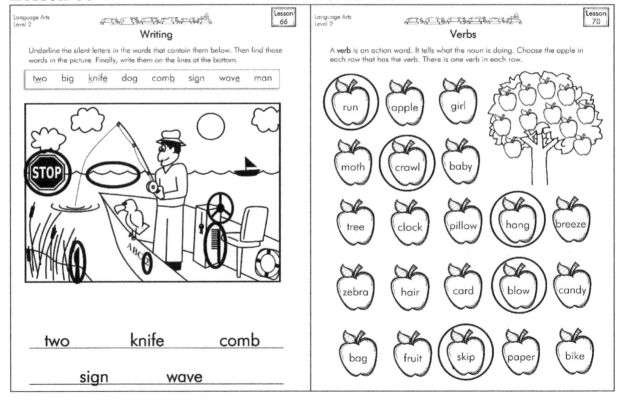

two   knife   comb

          sign   wave

Lesson 70

Verbs

A **verb** is an action word. It tells what the noun is doing. Choose the apple in each row that has the verb. There is one verb in each row.

run   apple   girl

moth   crawl   baby

tree   clock   pillow   hang   breeze

zebra   hair   card   blow   candy

bag   fruit   skip   paper   bike

Lesson 71

Spelling

Unscramble the words below. You can use the pictures on the page if you get stuck.

y b b a   <u>baby</u>

g d o   <u>dog</u>

s f i h   <u>fish</u>

a p n   <u>pan</u>

r i g l   <u>girl</u>

d b r i   <u>bird</u>

Lesson 72

Writing

Try to write this sentence in proper English. Read it out loud to help you figure out what it says: *Ah have mo' important things to worry about.*

I have more important things to worry about.

Verbs

Remember that verbs show action. Can you find 10 verbs in the words below? Circle them, or color them if you'd like.

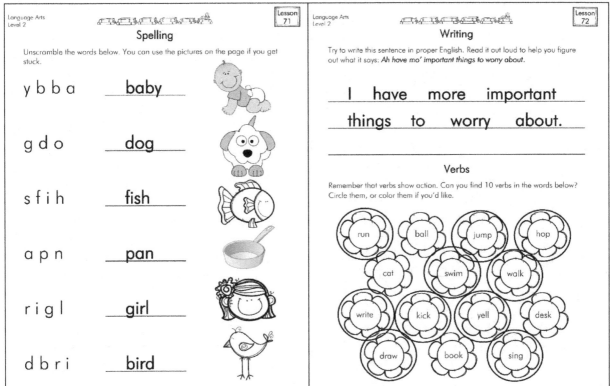

run   ball   jump   hop   cat   swim   walk   write   kick   yell   desk   draw   book   sing

Lesson 73

Writing

Copy this sentence: *Buster Bear could squash me by just stepping on me, but he doesn't try it.*

Buster Bear could squash me by just stepping on me, but he doesn't try it.

Plurals

Write the plural in the blank beside each word.

place <u>places</u>   tax <u>taxes</u>

match <u>matches</u>   lady <u>ladies</u>

mess <u>messes</u>   wife <u>wives</u>

Lesson 74

Action Verbs

Each line contains one action verb. Circle it.

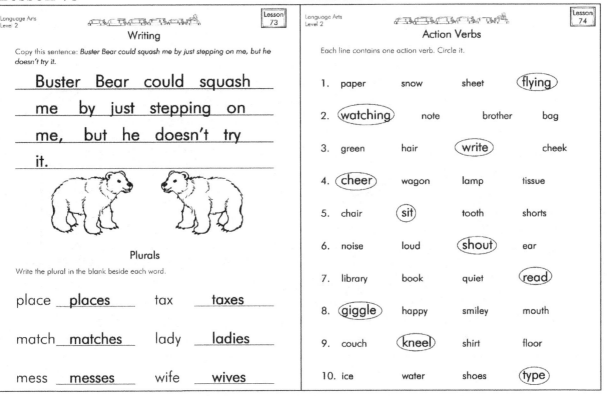

1. paper   snow   sheet   (flying)
2. (watching)   note   brother   bag
3. green   hair   (write)   cheek
4. (cheer)   wagon   lamp   tissue
5. chair   (sit)   tooth   shorts
6. noise   loud   (shout)   ear
7. library   book   quiet   (read)
8. (giggle)   happy   smiley   mouth
9. couch   (kneel)   shirt   floor
10. ice   water   shoes   (type)

Lesson 77

Verb Fishing

Circle or color all of the verb fish below.

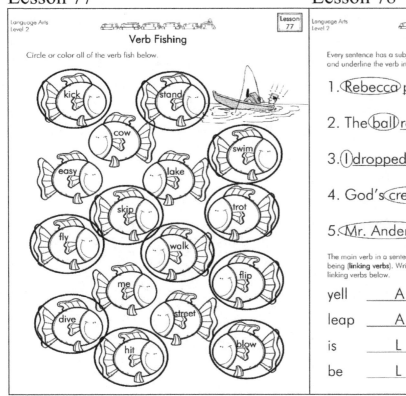

kick
stand
cow
swim
easy
lake
skip
trot
fly
walk
me
flip
dive
street
hit
blow

Lesson 78

Verb Types

Every sentence has a subject (a person or a thing) and a verb. Circle the subject and underline the verb in each of the following sentences.

1. Rebecca painted a beautiful picture.

2. The ball rolled down the hill.

3. I dropped my book.

4. God's creation is magnificent.

5. Mr. Anderson teaches math.

The main verb in a sentence either shows action (**action verbs**) or a state of being (**linking verbs**). Write an A next to the action verbs and an L next to the linking verbs below.

yell	A	are	L
leap	A	want	A
is	L	slept	A
be	L	was	L

Lesson 79

Verbs

Remember that verbs show action or a state of being. Circle the verbs in each sentence. Some sentences have more than one!

The phone rang.

The blue van was really loud.

The car raced down the street.

The cat chased after the mouse.

My favorite color is bright green.

There was nothing good on TV.

The cow jumped over the moon.

We were surprised when we heard the news.

The concert was excellent, so I clapped.

Are you circling all of the verbs?

We skipped rope for PE today.

How high can you throw a ball?

They cancelled the class because the speaker was sick.

Lesson 82

Find the Verbs

Uncover the hidden picture! If the word is a verb, color the space orange. If it is not a verb, color the space gray.

whisper   salad
star   car
                throw
                        chomp
space   spin
            look   think
                                gold
earth   laugh
                    cry
pen   belt
            send
cup   doctor

Can you think of 8 more verbs? Write them below. Do 4 of them!

_____   _____

_____ (answers will vary)

_____   _____

_____   _____

Lesson 83

Action Verbs

Remember that action verbs tell what someone or something does. They show action. Circle the action verbs in each of the sentences below.

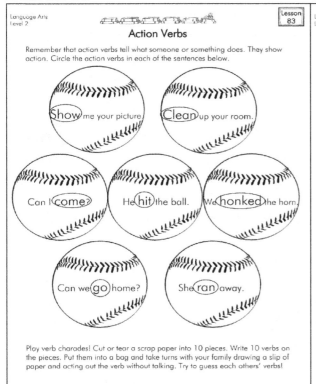

(Show) me your picture.

(Clean) up your room.

Can I (come)?

He (hit) the ball.

We (honked) the horn.

Can we (go) home?

She (ran) away.

Play verb charades! Cut or tear a scrap paper into 10 pieces. Write 10 verbs on the pieces. Put them into a bag and take turns with your family drawing a slip of paper and acting out the verb without talking. Try to guess each others' verbs!

Lesson 84

To Be

The verb *to be* is a verb that shows a state of being. Use the chart to fill in the missing form of *to be* in each sentence.

Person	Past	Present	Future
I	was	am	will be
you, they, we	were	are	will be
he, she, it	was	is	will be

Uncle Bob __was__ home, but now he's not.

The ball __is__ flat now since it hit a nail.

Tomorrow it __will be__ hot.

Yesterday it __was__ cold.

I __will be__ going to the store later.

They __were__ loud, but now they __are__ quiet.

It __is__ a beautiful day, isn't it?

You __will be__ coming over later.

Lesson 85

Writing

Write a sentence that is a question. What punctuation mark should go at the end? Then write an answer that is an exclamation. What punctuation mark should go at the end?

_____

_____

_____

_____

_____

Circle the flowers that contain linking verbs.

is   ball   was   floor

mop   are   cat

am   will be   soft   were

Lesson 91

Spelling

Find the *oi* words in the puzzle below.

```
W R K K O I L S Y J P R F T J
V P W P B I G E S G Y J N A M
X V B Q O B W S O I L M Z B I
E S M W I S H E S F U C O L B
O M N J N P J O I N T S B E O
C F O T G O U E I F Z P L S I
O R I L F I S T O I L B L R L
I K S Y Y N H K Y U W N E K L
L N E S F T J O I N W L A W Z
E I E T X L L N S A O S V K B
V V S M O W V S X I Y J E D A
H E Y B F D E O E C Z D S D B
U S F O I L S G R O V N Y N I
I A J V J F I G C I I X Q H E
W Q E V L I A B I N E S Y W S
```

oil	join	foil
boil	coin	toil
coil	joint	boing
soil	point	noise

Lesson 92

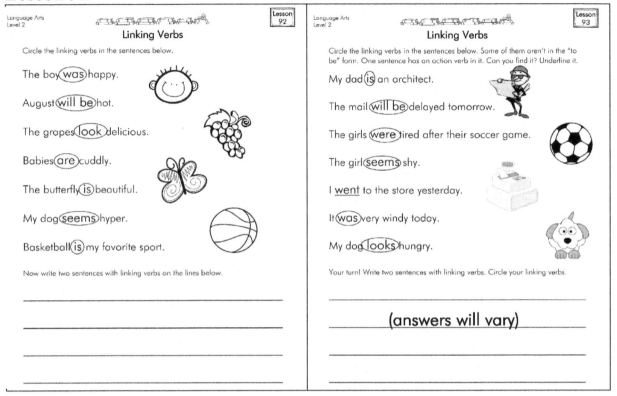

Linking Verbs

Circle the linking verbs in the sentences below.

The boy (was) happy.

August (will be) hot.

The grapes (look) delicious.

Babies (are) cuddly.

The butterfly (is) beautiful.

My dog (seems) hyper.

Basketball (is) my favorite sport.

Now write two sentences with linking verbs on the lines below.

_____

_____

_____

_____

Lesson 93

Linking Verbs

Circle the linking verbs in the sentences below. Some of them aren't in the "to be" form. One sentence has an action verb in it. Can you find it? Underline it.

My dad (is) an architect.

The mail (will be) delayed tomorrow.

The girls (were) tired after their soccer game.

The girl (seems) shy.

I <u>went</u> to the store yesterday.

It (was) very windy today.

My dog (looks) hungry.

Your turn! Write two sentences with linking verbs. Circle your linking verbs.

_____

(answers will vary)

_____

_____

Lesson 95

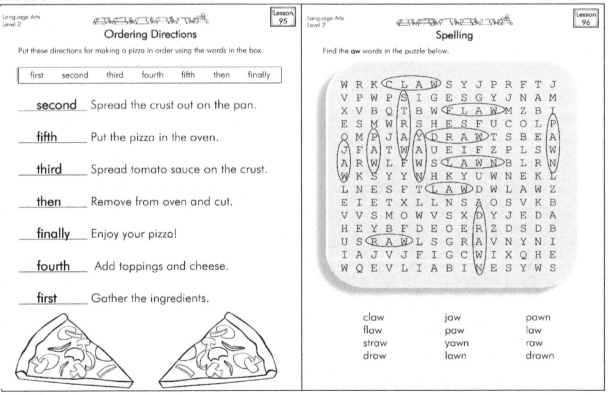

Ordering Directions

Put these directions for making a pizza in order using the words in the box.

| first | second | third | fourth | fifth | then | finally |

___second___ Spread the crust out on the pan.

___fifth___ Put the pizza in the oven.

___third___ Spread tomato sauce on the crust.

___then___ Remove from oven and cut.

___finally___ Enjoy your pizza!

___fourth___ Add toppings and cheese.

___first___ Gather the ingredients.

Lesson 96

Spelling

Find the **aw** words in the puzzle below.

```
W R K C L A W S Y J P R F T J
V P W P S I G E S G Y J N A M
X V B Q T B W F L A W M Z B I
E S M W R S H E S F U C O L P
Q M P J A Y D R A W T S B E A
J F A T W A U E I F Z P L S W
A R W L F W S L A W N B L R N
W K S Y Y W H K Y U W N E K L
L N E S F T L A W D W L A W Z
E I E T X L L N S A O S V K B
V V S M O W V S X D Y J E D A
H E Y B F D E O E R Z D S D B
U S R A W L S G R A V N Y N I
I A J V J F I G C W I X Q H E
W Q E V L I A B I N E S Y W S
```

claw	jaw	pawn
flaw	paw	law
straw	yawn	raw
draw	lawn	drawn

Lesson 97

Matching

Cut out the squares, mix them up and lay them face down on the table. Play a matching game where you match the sentences to either the **past tense** (already happened) or **future tense** (will happen later) of the verb in parentheses at the bottom. **(The correct answers are to the right of the sentences)**

We ___ cards last night. (play)	played	We ___ golf next week. (play)	will play
We ___ up the answer when we weren't sure. (look)	looked	Later tonight we ___ at the stars. (look)	will look
Last Christmas I ___ most of my relatives. (see)	saw	We ___ the new movie when it comes out. (see)	will see

Copy this sentence: *"The bride looked like a queen."* Do you think that's a nice way to describe her? Is it better than saying she looked pretty? What image do you picture?

"The bride looked like a queen."

Lesson 98

Past Tense

Verbs in the **past tense** are showing that something already happened. To make most verbs past tense, you simply add "ed" to the end. There are some exceptions to this. Read the examples and then make the verbs past tense.

If a verb ends in e, simply add "d" instead of "ed" (bake — baked).

| race | raced | please | pleased |
| tame | tamed | fake | faked |

If a verb ends in a consonant followed by a y, change the y to an i and then add "ed." If it ends in a vowel followed by a y, leave the y and add "ed." This is similar to the plural rule for words ending in y (carry — carried, play — played).

| hurry | hurried | obey | obeyed |
| cry | cried | stay | stayed |

Make these verbs past tense.

place	placed	jump	jumped
dry	dried	wash	washed
color	colored	clean	cleaned
enjoy	enjoyed	ask	asked
like	liked	try	tried
guess	guessed	worry	worried

Lesson 99

Ordering Sentences

Put these words in the order that makes a complete sentence. Add proper punctuation.

makes   Jane   dinner

Jane   makes   dinner.

laundry   folded   Mom

Mom   folded   laundry.

will order   We   pizza

We   will   order   pizza.

Pick the answer that best fits the sentence. Remember that each sentence needs a subject noun and predicate verb.

The dog _____.
a. drove a car
(b.) dug a hole
c. flew a plane

_____ flew in a line.
a. The cars
b. Scott
(c.) The birds

The ball _____.
a. smiled
b. green
(c.) rolled

_____ was tasty.
a. The bear
(b.) The drink
c. The sky

Lesson 101

Writing

Copy this sentence, *"But why do you carry that door?" asked the sheriff.* Make sure you write all of the punctuation. There are quotation marks showing that someone is speaking. There is a question mark showing that he is asking a question. There is a period to end the sentence. Also watch your spelling.

"But why do you carry that door?" asked the sheriff.

Spelling

Find the **er** words in the puzzle below.

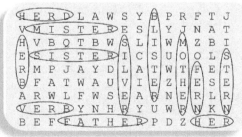

her	stern	mister
verb	fern	blister
silver	herb	mother
sister	herd	father

Lesson 102

Action Verbs

For each sentence, find the action verb and write it in the blank.

We went to the store early Friday morning. **went**

We put the groceries into the shopping cart. **put**

We had to wait at the checkout for a long time. **wait**

We finally paid the cashier for our groceries. **paid**

We then loaded our car with all of the groceries. **loaded**

We carefully drove home for a late lunch. **drove**

Which word is the action verb in each sentence?

I read the whole book.
(a.) read   c. whole
b. book   d. the

My dad grilled our burgers.
a. dad   c. burgers
b. my   (d.) grilled

She sat on the cold bench.
a. cold   (c.) sat
b. bench   d. on

We went to the beach.
a. beach   c. to
(b.) went   d. we

The bag hung on the hook.
a. hook   (c.) hung
b. bag   d. on

The ice cracked in the glass.
(a.) cracked   c. in
b. ice   d. glass

Lesson 103

Linking Verbs

For each sentence, find the linking verb and write it in the blank.

That girl seems nice and friendly to me. **seems**

All the kids who come look so happy. **look**

She was so hungry she wanted seconds. **was**

Harold is an award-winning sushi chef. **is**

Her shoes are the muddiest I've ever seen. **are**

My dad is thirsty and is asking for iced tea. **is/is**

Which word is the verb in each sentence?

We were late for church.
a. late   c. church
b. we   (d.) were

My sister has been sick.
a. My   (c.) has been
b. sister   d. sick

The baby is hungry.
a. the   (c.) is
b. baby   d. hungry

She feels very cold.
a. She   (c.) feels
b. very   d. cold

His room was a mess.
a. his   c. mess
(b.) was   d. room

They will be here tomorrow.
a. tomorrow   (c.) will be
b. here   d. they

Lesson 104

Verb Tense

The verb tense places a verb in time. The three main tenses are **past tense** (already happened), **present tense** (happening right now), and **future tense** (will happen later). Use the chart to help you fill in the right verb for each sentence. If you're having trouble, read the sentence out loud with each choice. The one that sounds right is probably the right one. Put a star next to the sentence in **present tense**.

Past	Present	Future
I baked cupcakes.	I bake cupcakes.	I will bake cupcakes.
I was baking cupcakes.	I am baking cupcakes.	I will be baking cupcakes.
I had been baking cupcakes.	I have been baking cupcakes.	I am going to bake cupcakes.

We **will go** to church tomorrow.
(went/will go)

I **rode** my bike yesterday.
(rode/ride)

☆My sister **is sleeping** right now.
(slept/is sleeping)

Yesterday, we **ate** pancakes.
(eat/ate)

I **will follow** God forever.
(followed/will follow)

Lesson 106

Spelling

Put an X over the cloud in each row that contains the misspelled word.

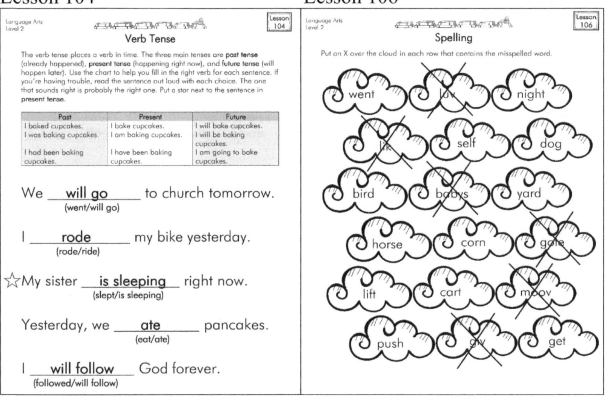

Lesson 107

Verb Tense

Write the correct tense of the action verb to match the rest of the sentence. **(There are additional forms of particularly the future tense that are acceptable answers.)**

(to dig) Yesterday, my dog __dug__ a hole.

(to sing) I __will sing__ a solo next week.

(to write) I __wrote__ a poem last night.

(to sleep) She __is sleeping__ right now.

(to play) Later, we __will play__ outside.

(to cook) Whenever he __cooks__, I eat well.

(to watch) We __are watching__ the game now.

(to run) I __ran__ a race last week.

(to eat) I __ate__ too much earlier.

(to sit) Next time, I __will sit__ beside you.

(to kick) Watch! She __kicks__ the ball hard.

(to fly) That bird always __flies__ at night.

Lesson 108

Writing

Copy any sentence from a book you are reading. What is the subject? What did the subject do (what is the predicate)? Make sure to start your sentence with a capital letter and end it with punctuation.

_____

(answers will vary)

_____

Subjects and Verbs

Circle the subject and underline the verbs in the sentences below.

After breakfast, (Justin) cleaned the table.

The shy little (girl) hugged her mom's leg.

The hyper (puppy) dropped his ball at my feet.

The (food) was piping hot.

(Sandra) forgot her flute for band rehearsal.

(William) ran the ball up the field.

Lesson 109

Predicates

The complete **predicate** is anything that isn't the subject – it tells what the subject of the sentence does. Underline the complete predicate in each sentence below.

Riley swept the kitchen.

Andrew rode his bike.

Olivia threw the ball.

The surfer caught the big wave.

The phone rang loudly.

The pig rolled in the mud.

The rainbow appeared over the clouds.

The dishwasher cleaned the dishes.

My mom went to the store.

Lesson 112

Writing

Copy this sentence. It's a little tricky! _"The man who has made up his mind to win," said Napoleon, "will never say impossible."_ Be careful to use commas and quotation marks to show someone is speaking. There are also two capital letters in this sentence.

"The   man   who   has   made

up   his   mind   to   win,"

said   Napoleon,   "will   never

say   impossible."

Linking Verbs

Circle the linking verbs below.

is   ball   was   shoe   it

were   will be   that   am

Lesson 113

Capitalization and Punctuation

Correct the sentences by underlining the words that should be capitalized and adding any missing punctuation.

<u>my</u> dog is so silly when he chases his tail<u>.</u>

<u>mr. robinson</u> was my favorite teacher.

<u>have</u> you ever been to another country<u>?</u>

<u>watch</u> out for that patch of ice<u>!</u>

<u>we</u> went to <u>alabama</u> last <u>tuesday</u>.

Writing

Copy this sentence. *At first the Romans, who were very proud and brave, did not think there was much danger.* Make sure you use two capital letters and two commas.

At first the Romans, who were very proud and brave, did not think there was much danger.

Lesson 114

Contractions

In the first section, choose the correct meaning of the contraction. In the second section, write the correct meaning of the contraction. In the last section, try to write the correct contraction for the words given.

we'll
a. they will   c. will not
(b.) we will   d. we are

haven't
a. do not   c. has not
b. will not   (d.) have not

you're
a. I am   (c.) you are
b. I will   d. you have

I've
(a.) I have   c. could have
b. we have   d. have not

I'll ___ **I will**   we've ___ **we have**

he'll ___ **he will**   don't ___ **do not**

didn't ___ **did not**   aren't ___ **are not**

I'm ___ **I am**   you'll ___ **you will**

were not ___ **weren't**

should have ___ **should've**

Lesson 117

Writing

Copy this sentence. *Nearly two thousand years ago there lived in Rome a man whose name was Julius Caesar.* Make sure you use capital letters in the right place and make sure you spell his name correctly.

Nearly two thousand years ago there lived in Rome a man whose name was Julius Caesar.

Action Verbs

Circle the action verbs below.

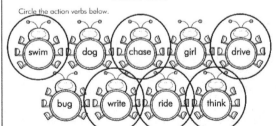

swim   dog   chase   girl   drive
bug   write   ride   think

Lesson 118

Capitalization and Punctuation

Underline the words that need to be capitalized and add the missing punctuation. For the final sentence, rewrite it correctly on the lines.

<u>the</u> teacher's name was <u>mr. king</u>.

<u>i</u> asked <u>michelle</u> to come with me to <u>chicago</u>.

<u>why</u> is it so cold today?

<u>my</u> favorite park is <u>central park</u>.

<u>we</u> went to <u>new york</u> last week and it was so crowded!

<u>are</u> you going to <u>metropolis zoo</u> with us on <u>friday</u>?

<u>watch</u> out for that angry dog!

<u>aunt cathy</u> and <u>i</u> are going <u>christmas</u> shopping.

can you help me make lunch for timothy

Can you help me make lunch for Timothy?

Lesson 119

Ordering Directions

Put these directions for making a snowman in order using the words in the box.

first	second	third	then	finally

then Stack the three balls largest to smallest.

second Make the next ball slightly smaller.

first Roll a large ball for the base of your snowman.

finally Add eyes, nose, mouth, and arms.

third Make the last ball the smallest of all.

Put these directions for making scrambled eggs in order using the words in the box.

first	second	third	fourth	fifth	then	finally

fourth Whisk the cracked eggs and milk in the bowl.

then Cook over medium heat until done.

finally Serve with toast and enjoy!

second Crack the eggs into the bowl.

third Pour a splash of milk into the bowl of eggs.

fifth Pour the whisked eggs into the pan.

first Gather the eggs, whisk, milk, bowl, and pan.

Lesson 122

Writing

Write the name: **Alexander the Great.**

Alexander   the   Great

Possessive Nouns

Choose the noun that shows possession. Things like the dog's bone, the house's door, the girl's hair - these all show possession. Notice the 's? Circle the choice that best fits in the blank.

The _____ melody was catchy.
songs'   (song's)

The _____ voice was scratchy.
(boy's)   boys'

The _____ tire was flat.
(bike's)   bikes'

The _____ claws were sharp.
cats'   (cat's)

My _____ pages are worn.
books'   (book's)

Lesson 123

Possessive Nouns

Circle the choice that best fits the blank.

The _____ frosting was delicious.
cupcakes'   (cupcake's)

The _____ sail was colorful.
(boat's)   boats'

The _____ laugh was adorable.
(baby's)   babies'

Writing

Write the name of five people in your family. Now make them each own something by adding 's. For example: *Mom's computer.*

_____

_____

(answers will vary)

_____

_____

_____

Lesson 124

Plural Possessive Nouns

When a noun is plural or ends in an s and you want to make it possessive, in most cases you add the apostrophe after the s like this s'. For example James' shirt, the girls' dresses (this is more than one girl), the boys' games (this is more than one boy). Circle the correct answer for each sentence. Is it plural? Is it possessive?

The three _____ clothes matched.
(girls')   girl's

The two _____ stars were red.
(balls')   ball's

Her _____ names were Rex and Max.
dog's   (dogs')

The seven _____ backs were gray.
chair's   (chairs')

_____ car was red.
(James')   Jame's

Writing

Write this: *Genghis Khan's hawk.*

Genghis   Khan's   hawk

Lesson 125

Its/It's

When it is possessive, you do not use an apostrophe. When you use an apostrophe in the word, you turn it into a contraction that means "it is." Circle the form of it that best fits each sentence. Then write two sentences at the bottom. One should use *its* and mean that something belongs to it. The other should use *it's* and mean it is.

The dog got _____ fur muddy.
(its)   it's

_____ really hot outside today.
Its   (It's)

I think _____ fun to play in the rain.
its   (it's)

_____ house is a hole in the wall.
(Its)   It's

_____

(answers will vary)

_____

_____

Lesson 127

Its/It's

Circle the form of it that best fits each sentence. Then write two new sentences at the bottom. One should use *its* and mean that something belongs to it. The other should use *it's* and mean it is.

It was so old _____ paint was flaking off.
(its)   it's

_____ a beautiful rainbow!
Its   (It's)

That's a pretty color. What is _____ name?
(its)   it's

_____ Friday today.
Its   (It's)

_____

(answers will vary)

_____

_____

Lesson 128

Proofreading

Correct the sentences! The mistakes have been underlined. Do you know how to correct them? Write the corrected sentence on the lines.

My aunt, uncle, en cousins is visiting today

My aunt, uncle, and cousins are visiting today.

They always brings they're dogs

They always bring their dogs.

the dog's names are max and titan.

The dogs' names are Max and Titan.

Do you have a fun ant en uncle, too.

Do you have a fun aunt and uncle, too?

Lesson 137

Subject Pronouns

Use the chart below to fill in the missing subject pronouns from the sentences. (You probably don't even need the chart, but it's there if you do!)

Person	Singular	Plural
1st (speaking)	I	we
2nd (spoken to)	you	you
3rd (spoken about)	he/she/it	they

(Meg, Jill, and I) **We** played ball together.

(Your dad) **He** works hard at his job.

([Speaking to] Tom) **You** are being too loud.

(The dog and cat) **They** chased each other.

(Philadelphia) **It** is a city rich in history.

(You and I) **We** are on the same team.

(Jack and Tom) **They** are on the other team.

(My Aunt Sally) **She** is a nurse.

(The apple) **It** was sweet.

(My brother) **He** likes sweet apples.

Lesson 138

Object Pronouns

Use the chart below to fill in the missing object pronouns from the sentences. (You probably don't even need the chart, but it's there if you do!)

Person	Singular	Plural
1st (speaking)	me	us
2nd (spoken to)	you	you
3° (spoken about)	him/her/it	them

Brian wanted to play with __us__. (Meg, Jill, and me)

You must really love __him__. (Your dad)

I am talking to __you__. ([Speaking to] Tom)

I tried to keep up with __them__. (The dog and cat)

Last year, we visited __it__. (Philadelphia)

The coach seems to like __us__. (You and me)

I hope we don't lose to __them__. (Jack and Tom)

The other nurses really like __her__. (My Aunt Sally)

The orange wasn't sweet like __it__. (The apple)

Apples taste better to __him__. (My brother)

Lesson 139

Subject and Object Pronouns

Is the missing pronoun a subject or an object pronoun? Write the correct form of the pronoun in the blank.

I wanted to play with __her__, but she was busy.
she/her

You must really love your dad. __He__ works hard.
He/Him

I tried to keep up with __them__, but they kept running.
they/them

You and I will have fun if the coach puts __us__ in.
we/us

Jack and Tom are good. __They__ will be hard to beat.
They/Them

My Aunt Sally is kind, so the other nurses like __her__.
she/her

My Aunt Sally thinks __they__ are kind too.
they/them

My mom went to the store. __She__ forgot her list.
She/Her

Lesson 141

Word Builder

Choose the letters from the box that best fit the blanks within the sentences. Write them in your neatest handwriting. Write each completed word again on the lines at the bottom of the page.

| co | ag | ace | it | gy | oal |

I scored a g_oal_ in last week's soccer game.

I don't mean to br_ag_, but my mom is the best!

Our c_it_y got a new mayor.

The _co_t was hard and cold.

The look on her f_ace_ was happy.

My dad and I went to the _gy_m to shoot some hoops.

goal   brag   city   cot

face   gym

Lesson 142

Contractions

Find which tree the contraction apple goes to. Remember that the apostrophe represents a missing letter or letters. That can help you figure out the meaning. Draw a line from the apple to the right tree.

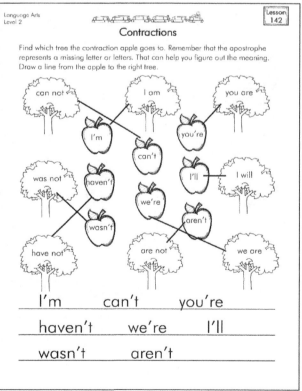

I'm   can't   you're

haven't   we're   I'll

wasn't   aren't

Lesson 143

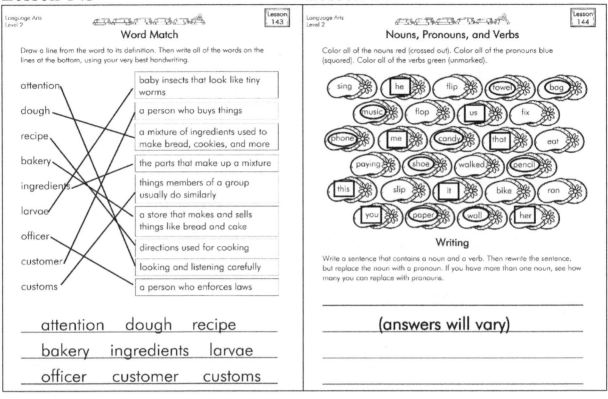

Word Match

Draw a line from the word to its definition. Then write all of the words on the lines at the bottom, using your very best handwriting.

attention

dough

recipe

bakery

ingredients

larvae

officer

customer

customs

baby insects that look like tiny worms
a person who buys things
a mixture of ingredients used to make bread, cookies, and more
the parts that make up a mixture
things members of a group usually do similarly
a store that makes and sells things like bread and cake
directions used for cooking
looking and listening carefully
a person who enforces laws

attention   dough   recipe

bakery   ingredients   larvae

officer   customer   customs

Lesson 144

Nouns, Pronouns, and Verbs

Color all of the nouns red (crossed out). Color all of the pronouns blue (squared). Color all of the verbs green (unmarked).

sing · he · flip · towel · bag · music · flop · us · fix · phone · me · candy · that · eat · paying · shoe · walked · pencil · this · slip · it · bike · ran · you · paper · wall · her

Writing

Write a sentence that contains a noun and a verb. Then rewrite the sentence, but replace the noun with a pronoun. If you have more than one noun, see how many you can replace with pronouns.

(answers will vary)

Lesson 146

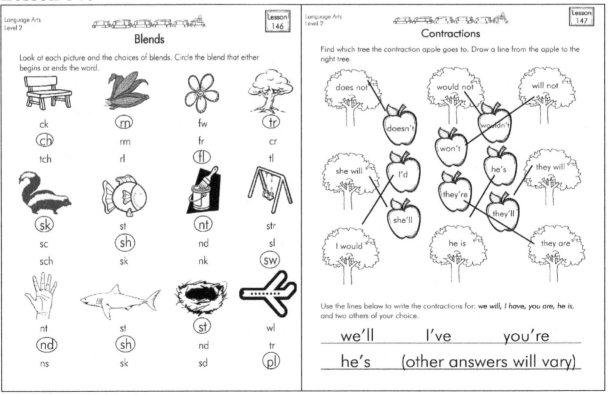

Blends

Look at each picture and the choices of blends. Circle the blend that either begins or ends the word.

ck / (ch) / tch

(rn) / rm / rl

fw / fr / (fl)

(tr) / cr / tl

(sk) / sc / sch

st / (sh) / sk

(nt) / nd / nk

str / sl / (sw)

nt / (nd) / ns

st / (sh) / sk

(st) / nd / sd

wl / tr / (pl)

Lesson 147

Contractions

Find which tree the contraction apple goes to. Draw a line from the apple to the right tree.

does not · would not · will not
doesn't · wouldn't · won't
she will · I'd · he's · they will
they're · they'll
I would · he is · they are
she'll

Use the lines below to write the contractions for: *we will, I have, you are, he is,* and two others of your choice.

we'll   I've   you're

he's   (other answers will vary)

Lesson 148

Spelling Suffixes

Using the words in the box, write each word next to its definition. Be sure to write as neatly as you can. Can you figure out what each **suffix** or word ending means based on the common definitions?

> bravely   slowly   sadly   cheerful   hopeful
> fearless   useless   kindness   loudness

full of cheer **cheerful**

without use **useless**

in a way that is brave **bravely**

being loud **loudness**

in a way that is sad **sadly**

full of hope **hopeful**

without fear **fearless**

in a way that is slow **slowly**

being kind **kindness**

Lesson 149

Word Builder

Choose the letters from the box that best fit the blanks within the sentences. Write them in your neatest handwriting. Do you hear a common sound in the finished words? Write each completed word on the lines at the bottom of the page.

> og   lo   all   ra   ta   aw

I needed to c **all** my mom when I was ready to be picked up.

My d **og** is the smartest one on the planet.

I love to d **ra** w pictures for my dad.

I tripped on a **lo** g on our hike.

I s **aw** a frog on our porch.

My brother is so **ta** ll he can touch the ceiling.

call   dog   draw   log

saw   tall

Lesson 151

Word Match

Draw a line from the word to its definition. Then write all of the words on the lines at the bottom, using your very best handwriting.

fussed	two feelers on the head of an insect
penalty	helpful or beneficial
grumpily	gave their word that they would do something
groaned	mad
antennae	complained in an angry or disgruntled way
grumbled	punishment for disobeying some sort of rule
promised	protested or complained
advantage	acting in a grumpy way
angry	made a moaning sound

fussed   penalty   grumpily

groaned   antennae   grumbled

promised   advantage   angry

Lesson 152

Writing

Copy this sentence: *"I'm afraid I don't know how,"* replied the country lad. Pay attention to all of the punctuation and capitalization.

"I'm   afraid   I   don't   know how,"   replied   the   country lad.

What are the two contractions in the sentence?

I'm   don't

What do the contractions mean?

I am   do not

Can you find a pronoun in the sentence?

I

Can you find a common noun in the sentence?

lad

Lesson 153

Writing

Copy this sentence: *"I'll have to teach Danny Rugg a good lesson," said Bert to his cousin.* Pay attention to all of the punctuation and capitalization.

"I'll have to teach Danny Rugg a good lesson," said Bert to his cousin.

What is the contraction in the sentence?

I'll

What does the contraction mean?

I will

Can you find a pronoun in the sentence?

his

Can you find any proper nouns in the sentence?

Danny Rugg   Bert

Lesson 154

Writing

Copy this sentence: *"That's what we'll do!" cried Bert, steering toward it.* Pay attention to all of the punctuation and capitalization.

"That's what we'll do!" cried Bert, steering toward it.

There is an 's word in the sentence. Is it possessive or a contraction?

contraction

What does it mean?

That is

Can you find a pronoun in the sentence?

it

Can you find a proper noun in the sentence?

Bert

Lesson 157

Word Builder

Choose the letters from the box that best fit the blanks within the sentences. Write them in your neatest handwriting. Write each completed word on the lines at the bottom of the page.

| ew | ot | ok | bl | oo | ou |

The wind __bl__ ew so hard it knocked over my bicycle.

My father's bo__ot__ was so muddy it left tracks all over the floor.

The m__oo__n is full and beautiful tonight.

I got some n__ew__ shoes yesterday.

It to__ok__ a week but I finished the whole book.

I hope y__ou__ have a great day!

blew   boot   moon   new

took   you

Lesson 158

Word Match

Draw a line from the word to its definition. Then write all of the words on the lines at the bottom, using your very best handwriting.

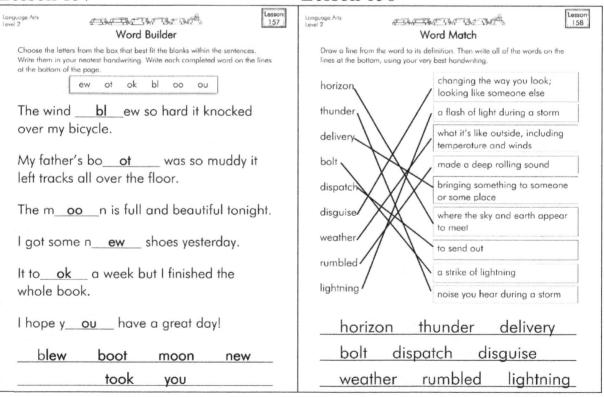

horizon	changing the way you look; looking like someone else
thunder	a flash of light during a storm
delivery	what it's like outside, including temperature and winds
bolt	made a deep rolling sound
dispatch	bringing something to someone or some place
disguise	where the sky and earth appear to meet
weather	to send out
rumbled	a strike of lightning
lightning	noise you hear during a storm

horizon   thunder   delivery

bolt   dispatch   disguise

weather   rumbled   lightning

Lesson 159

Writing

Copy this sentence: *Then came another thaw, and a freeze followed some days later, making good skating.*

Then came another thaw, and a freeze followed some days later, making good skating.

Can you find a plural noun in the sentence?

days

Can you find the two past tense verbs?

came   followed

Can you find the present tense verb?

making

Lesson 161

Vowel Pairing

Use the apples to pick the vowels that are missing from each word. Write them in the blank.

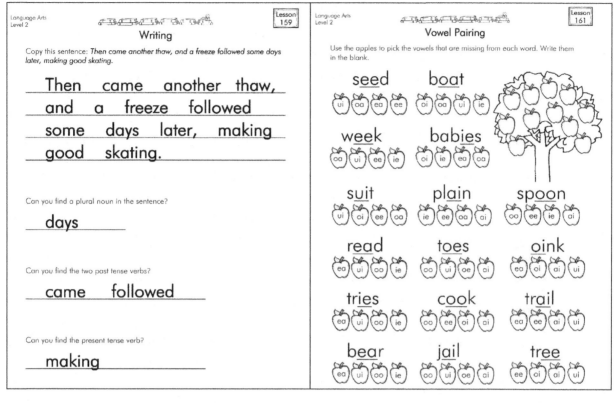

seed — ui oa ea ee
boat — oi oa ui ie

week — oa ui ee ie
babies — oi ie ea oa

suit — ui oi ee oa
plain — ie ee oa ai
spoon — oo ee ie ai

read — ea ui oo ie
toes — oo ui oe ai
oink — ea oi ai ui

tries — ea ui oo ie
cook — oo ee oi ai
trail — ea ee ai ui

bear — ea ui oo ie
jail — oo ui oe ai
tree — ee oi ai ui

Lesson 162

Grammar

Write which of the two underlined words answer the question for each sentence. Be careful! Some of the words can be both nouns and verbs, so the context of the sentence is important to decide which way they are being used.

Which word is the verb?

I practiced my flute.

practiced

Which word is the noun?

I went to soccer practice.

practice

Which word is the noun?

The dog barked.

dog

Which word is the verb?

My shoe is untied.

is

Which word is the verb?

He jumped off the swing.

jumped

Which word is the noun?

She swung from the tree.

tree

Which word is the verb?

The ball rolled downhill.

rolled

Which word is the verb?

The roll was delicious.

was

Which word is the noun?

We shopped all day.

day

Which word is the noun?

The shop felt cold.

shop

Lesson 163

Matching

These spelling words sound the same but are spelled differently. Read through the words and simplified definitions first – the definitions are to the right of the words. Then cut them out and mix them up. Play a matching game to help you learn which spelling word goes with which definition.

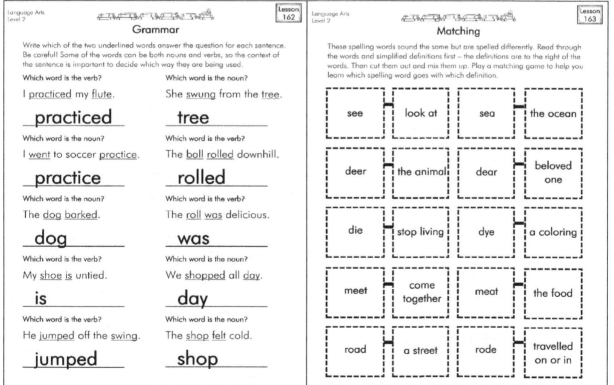

see	look at	sea	the ocean
deer	the animal	dear	beloved one
die	stop living	dye	a coloring
meet	come together	meat	the food
road	a street	rode	travelled on or in

Lesson 164

Spelling

Do you remember your spelling words? See if you can write the correct word beside each simplified definition from lesson 163.

__see__	look at
__sea__	the ocean
__deer__	the animal
__dear__	beloved one
__die__	stop living
__dye__	a coloring
__meet__	come together
__meat__	the food
__road__	a street
__rode__	travelled on or in

Lesson 165

Spelling Bee

Using your same words from the last two lessons, fill in the blanks below. If you need to check on a word or definition, you can use lesson 163 to help you.

I __see__ blue skies today.

The __sea__ is salty.

A __deer__ came into our yard last night.

My family is very __dear__ to me.

The leaves __die__ and fall in autumn.

We used green __dye__ on our project.

Can we __meet__ at the park?

Vegetarians don't eat __meat__.

The __road__ was full of traffic.

We __rode__ our bikes all weekend.

Lesson 178

Final Research Project

Practice your editing skills. Circle what's wrong in the sentences below.

(U)ncle (P)hil is a really good dancer.
(capitalize)

My mom likes to feed the (deer) in our backyard.
(homophone - deer)

(m)y brothers favorite sport is hockey.
(capitalize)   (missing apostrophe)

The three girls dresses all matched.
(apostrophe should follow the s)

The fo(x)s went to their den for some rest( )
(es follows x to make a plural) (missing period)

(o)ur coach stay(d) with us while we waited for (ore) parents.
(capitalize)(ed for past tense)(homophone – our)

The boys went home, but (i) helped dad finish his work(?)
(always capitalized)   (period)

Watch out( )The stove is very ho( )
(both periods would be better as exclamation points)

Lesson 180

Verb Review

Let's review verbs one last time! Color all of the linking verbs blue (circled). Color all of the action verbs green (left alone). All of the flowers should be colored when you are done.

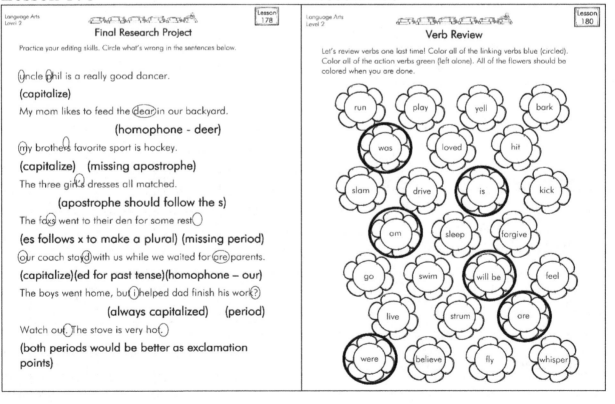

We hope you had a great year with EP Language Arts 2.

EP provides free, complete, high quality online homeschool curriculum for children around the world. Find more of our courses and resources on our site, allinonehomeschool.com.

If you prefer offline materials, consider Genesis Curriculum which takes a book of the Bible and turns it into daily lessons in science, social studies, and language arts for your children to learn all together. The curriculum also includes learning Biblical languages. Genesis Curriculum offers Rainbow Readers and A Mind for Math, a math curriculum designed for about first through fourth grade to be done all together. Each math lesson is based on the day's Bible reading from the main curriculum. GC Steps is an offline preschool and kindergarten program. Learn more about our expanding curriculum on our site, GenesisCurriculum.com.

Made in the USA
Monee, IL
18 September 2020